Commemorative Pottery 1780–1900

A Guide for Collectors

JOHN AND JENNIFER MAY

Commemorative Pottery 1780–1900

A Guide for Collectors

HEINEMANN : LONDON

William Heinemann Ltd
15 Queen St, Mayfair, London W1X 8BE

LONDON   MELBOURNE   TORONTO
JOHANNESBURG   AUCKLAND

First published 1972

434 45710 8

Photoset and printed in Great Britain by
BAS Printers Limited, Wallop, Hampshire

This book is for James

Contents

Preface and Acknowledgements

This book deals with British commemorative pottery from 1780 to 1900. It explains why these were the crucial years for this particular form of ceramic art. It subdivides the major events commemorated into rational and identifiable sections, lists some of the history behind the event and gives an idea of the sort of piece the reader may reasonably expect to find commemorating it. It is as lavishly illustrated as possible and, wherever possible, has been illustrated with items from private collections which, otherwise, the reader would never see. It also includes, however, a guide to the pieces on show in Britain's museums. These of course can always be seen by the collector and, if the curator is given advance warning, can often be examined out of the case or, more likely, exhumed from a storeroom. This last section will, the authors hope, in some way recompense for the many interesting local and less prestigious events and personalities that lack of space compelled them to omit.

It does not deal with portrait figures; these are very well dealt with in a book also published by Messrs Heinemann and written by that very considerable expert Anthony Oliver.

Nor does it deal with types of pottery; it assumes that the collector already has a working knowledge of pottery and can identify creamware and pearlware and underglaze and overglaze decoration, etc. If this is not the case, however, the authors warmly recommend *English and Scottish Earthenware* by G. Bernard Hughes as a first-class initiation into the intricacies of factories and fashions in pottery.

And now it remains only to thank our customers, who so freely gave access to their collections. And to hope that when the reader has finished this book he or she will feel that at long last a reasonably scholarly book has been produced on what is, without doubt, one of the most fascinating and rewarding aspects of ceramic collection.

𝕴 I 𝕴

The Sociological Background

The British have long commemorated their history in pottery. Kings and queens, great events, political struggles, victories and sometimes defeats, all have found their way on to mugs and jugs and plates and bowls.

The earliest of these pieces actually to be commemorative, as opposed simply to carrying the image of a king or queen or both, is a mug celebrating the coronation of Charles II in 1660 (although actually this was intended for some other event: the body is that of Oliver Cromwell and an ingenious artist has obviously and rather hastily changed the face). This mug is always on show at the London Museum, Kensington. It is, of course, made of delft.

But this mug is exceptional. And right the way through the reigns of William and Mary, Anne and the first two Georges there was very little commemorative pottery produced.

1. A very rare jug eulogizing the second Duke of Leinster, a man who though he may have been "universally beloved" di little to justify the production of such a generous epitaph. These jugs were probably distributed to the estate worke at the time of his funeral.

I

A very fine example of hand painting
early creamware. The pot was probably
de at the time of George III's
ronation. By courtesy of the City
iseum and Art Gallery, Stoke-on-Trent.

The transfer, which commemorates the
ce of Amiens, comes in two colours,
en and blue. Expert opinions ascribe
to Swansea and one to Liverpool, but
er as to which is which. (See also plate
, Naval and Military.)

Indeed it was not until the 1780s that there began to
trickle from the potteries the sort of commemorative piece
that was finally to culminate in the flood of ware for Queen
Victoria's Diamond Jubilee in 1897.

For this there was a number of interlocked reasons.

First and foremost there was no form of pottery suitable
for semi-mass-production. Slipware was entirely hand-potted.
Salt-glazed brown stoneware gave virtually no flexibility in
decoration. And white salt-glaze really very little more.
Delft was fragile and hard to work with; production of it was
slow and the breakage rate was high. And the same was true
of the 'primitive' pot bases of the earlier Astbury, Wood,
Whieldon periods.

Secondly, although 'applied' decoration was possible from
very early on, and moulding feasible from the 1730s, there
was no means of mass-producing surface decoration. Each
piece had to be treated as an individual effort, and though
the painters became very deft, output was still limited to
the individual output of a few men.

Thirdly, there was no adequate transportation system
either to bring the raw materials of potting cheaply to the

4. This creamware punch pot is the only piece recorded that commemorates the *contemporary* building of the famous and much celebrated Wear mouth or, Sunderland, Bridge. It is encaptioned "An East view of the Bridge *to be erected* across the River Ware".

potteries or to distribute the finished goods. Eighteenth-century roads were little if any improvement on medieval ones, and the number of navigable miles of river was strictly limited. Indeed, the only certain method of travel was coastal shipping; which helps to explain the positioning of the early potteries.

Fourthly, there was, for the same reasons, a very inadequate dissemination of news. And people could scarcely be expected cheerfully to purchase a pot commemorating an event they didn't even know had happened!

Fifthly, there was a small population, thinly spread in dispersed rural areas and with scant money to spare on such trivialities as these.

But, about 1780, this all changed.

First, came a new sort of pottery. In the very early 1760s, Josiah Wedgwood invented creamware.

Creamware allowed for fast production, little wastage, anyway compared to earlier wares, and far easier decoration. Above all it permitted a constancy of quality which made runs of production a really feasible proposition.

Wedgwood did not patent creamware or, as he called it,

5. Compare this comparatively early creamware bridge tankard with plate 4. It was, of course, made long after the bridge was opened, probably in the 182– Ware 'commemorating' the bridge is still being produced today.

A fine and very rare transfer of the
[...]der Brunel; not to be confused with his
[...]ore famous son Isambard Kingdom, who
[...]lt several early steam ships and was
[...]sponsible for the broad-gauge GWR
[...]ilway. Sir J. M. Brunel is perhaps best
[...]membered for his Thames Tunnel, a
[...]oject which is itself commemorated, most
[...]mmonly on children's plates. (See
[...]ate 24.)

Probably the most commemorated of
local elections was the infamous
[...]wick election of 1826. There were four
[...]didates, Bell, Liddell, Beaumont and
[...]rd Howick. The last withdrew almost
[...]mediately, Bell and Liddell being finally
[...]cted. The two successful candidates
[...]blished large quantities of mugs, jugs
[...]d bowls, presumably for presentation to
[...]ir supporters. This particular transfer
[...]ery rare, and unusual in that it features
four candidates.

Queen's ware. Indeed one of the points he made when he was
arguing against a monopoly of ingredients was specifically
that he had 'discovered the art of making Queen's ware,
which employs ten times more people than all the China in
the Kingdom and *did not ask for a patent* for this important
discovery'.

The result of Wedgwood's energy and altruistic attitude
was that, by the 1780s, and even more so by the 1790s, a
large number of potteries were turning out considerable
quantities of creamware and its kindred pearlware.

Wedgwood's development of creamware was almost
exactly paralleled by his inventions of, first, a black basalt
body in the 1760s, followed by his startling jasper bodies in
1774. These bodies were quickly copied by other potters and
from 1780 to well into the first quarter of the nineteenth
century a large number of such pieces were made. Frequent
use of these bodies, with moulded or applied figures, is made

in pieces commemorating the various Napoleonic War battles, both on land and at sea.

These advances were, in their turn, nearly paralleled by the production of another mass-production ware. In October 1809 Miles Mason of the Lane Delf pottery, Staffordshire, first offered for sale his stone-china, later, of course, to be developed into the famous Mason's patent Ironstone by his sons George and Charles James. Only five years later Josiah Spode II was marketing a very fine and durable stone-china indeed, and as early as 1800, a form of 'stone-china' was being introduced by William and John Turner of Lane End, Staffordshire.

So by the very early nineteenth century there were a great many forms of very hard, very easily worked wares available to the potters, from which they could quickly, efficiently and cheaply produce amongst many other forms of pottery an ever-increasing number and variety of commemorative pieces.

Secondly, and concurrently with the development of these various forms of body, a solution to the problem of decoration was being evolved.

8. Pieces made to commemorate Grace Darling are not particularly rare. But most were made at the time of her death in 1842: this particular transfer, however, could be contemporary with the rescue (1838) and as such, is much more unusual. It appears, always, on very well-potted Sunderland lustre jugs.

9. There are a great many transfers featuring the immensely popular founder of the Wesleyan movement. This one was probably first published at the time of the Methodist centenary, in 1839.

10. A very rare transfer, so far recorded only on this particular jug, featuring Richard Oastler "the Factory King", one of the campaigners for the ten hour factory bill. It was probably published either in 1832, when Oastler arranged a much publicized meeting at York, or ten years later, to raise money for the fund organized to release Oastler from a debtors' prison.

11. In 1864 the retaining walls of the huge new Bradfield reservoir above Sheffield collapsed, and the outskirts of the town were flooded. (The reservoir had held over a million cubic feet of water.) A number of mugs and plates with varying transfers of the results of the disaster were published and sold, probably to raise money for the survivors' fund. The Sheffield museum has a set on view. By courtesy of the Sheffield City Museum.

Caption on mug: OAKS COLLIERY SECOND EXPLOSION.

In 1756 John Sadler, a potter of Harrington Street, Liverpool, and son of Adam Sadler, a printer in the New Market, Liverpool, together with Guy Green, who succeeded Adam Sadler in the New Market, invented a method of applying transfer printing to earthenware as opposed to the then current practice of each piece being individually decorated by hand.

The process of transfer printing is really very simple and is much the same today as it was in the eighteenth century.

Very briefly: the design was cut deeply into a flat copper plate; this plate was then warmed and charged with the colour mixed with thick boiled oil; excess 'ink' was cleaned off and a sheet of thin but strong paper called 'pottery tissue', having been soaked in a weak solution of soap, was laid on the plate and pressed. The resultant transfer was then trimmed and applied firmly to the pot. Once it was fired, the piece was dunked into cold water and while the paper washed away, the 'ink', being oil, remained unaffected. The oil was then 'burnt-off' by placing the wares in a low-

7

13. On February the 2nd 1829 an unfortunate madman called Jonathan Martin set York Minster on fire. The damage done was very considerable and a patriotic fund was raised to pay for the restoration. This jug, with its dramatic transfer of the Minster in flames, was almost certainly sold to raise money for the fund.

14. The old Houses of Parliament burnt down on the night of October the 17th 1834. The event is marked only by this transfer, which occurs both on a mug, as shown here, and on a very finely potted children's plate. In both cases, the item falls into the 'very rare' category.

temperature, hardening-on kiln.

If the print was 'over the glaze' (that is, had been applied to the already glazed pot), that was the end of the process. If, however, as was always done in the later part of the early nineteenth century and frequently, particularly with blue printing, in the very late eighteenth century, the print was applied to the biscuit, the ware was then cooled, dipped into the glaze and fired in the glost kiln.

If what Sadler and Green claimed was true – and it was – that two men transfer printing could equal the output of one hundred decorators, it is not surprising that the process revolutionized the pottery industry. It was, indeed, the first real application of the principles of the industrial revolution and the switch from craftsman to artisan that the pottery industry had experienced.

At first the process remained centred upon Liverpool; but soon Wedgwood and other leading potters began to print their own wares. Certainly by the 1770s printers and engravers were well established in Liverpool, the Potteries, Swansea,

15. Father Matthew, the great Irish advocate of teetotalism, came to London in 1843 and preached to congregations of many thousands at a specially prepared site in the Commercial Road. This transfer was, undoubtedly, originally produced then. But it recurs in a series of octagonal children's plates (as illustrated here) which include other noted transfers of Victoria's reign including her Coronation, and which was very likely made in 1851 for sale around the Crystal Palace.

16. A particularly fine transfer of the Kensington Exhibition of 1862. This was a much recorded event and pieces commemorating it are not rare.

17. A very fine plate, blue-printed and lavishly gilded, made to commemorate W. G. Grace's century of centuries. It was published in 1895 by the Coalport Porcelain Works. In this century, Royal Worcester have published some fine cricketing commemoratives, carrying the signatures of various test teams – an interesting continuance of an idea from one century to the next.

18. It would be impossible to list the number of transfers produced to commemorate the Great Exhibition. This is one of the more rare. The figure in the foreground is often claimed to be the Duke of Wellington: there seems, however, little, if any, evidence to support this.

Bristol and indeed wherever any appreciable quantity of earthenware was being manufactured.

The result, of course, was a huge increase in production and a huge decrease in price. By the 1820s the process had grown so popular that it was far and away the largest method of decoration used. Starting with the production of very large quantities of 'blue-and-white' ware, the various potteries flooded the British, American and Continental markets with printing of every kind, in virtually every colour. (The widely held belief that only black and blue underglaze printing were possible before 1829 is wrong. In the authors' private collection is a Swansea jug, decorated in green underglaze with a most elaborate transfer, published to celebrate the Peace of Amiens in 1802.)

Finally, in 1848, the process was elaborated by F. W. Collins and A. Reynolds, who together patented a process by which three colours, blue, red and yellow, could be affixed from a single transfer with a single firing. This process was enthusiastically taken up by the firm of F. & R. Pratt of Fenton, who produced with it a wide and now famous range of pots and pot lids. Many of these, of course, carry commemorative subjects, such as the Crystal Palace and the Prince Consort; but it is doubtful whether they were genuine commemorative pieces, produced actually at the time of the happening, and certainly many of them were still being produced long after the original event was over.

Thirdly, and again roughly concurrent with the technical developments in potting and printing that made available much larger quantities of pieces at much more realistic prices, Britain's communication systems were being drastically revised. This meant that not only were the raw materials becoming available as never before and at prices that were more and more competitive, but the fragile, finished articles were able to be transported further and further afield at ever increasing speed in ever increasing safety.

This revision involved the quite separate and quite astonishing development of this country's three major communication methods: water, roads, and latterly, railroads.

Water communication began its metamorphosis in July 1761 with the opening of the Bridgewater Canal.

Some idea of the change that the canals would make to the economics of Britain can be appreciated from the fact that, once the canal was open, the price of coal in Manchester literally *halved*.

But, of course, canals meant more than just lower prices. They meant much less destructive transport, particularly important for pottery, far greater social activity and far swifter and more thorough dissemination of news. They heralded a nation who knew what was happening when it was happening, with the result that they made the production of commemorative pieces, both for celebratory and for propaganda purposes, infinitely more logical, appealing and, above all, acceptable. And, as a concept, they spread rapidly.

By 1830, the peak period for water travel, there were over 4,000 miles of canals and navigable rivers criss-crossing the country, 3,500 miles of which had been built since 1760.

19. Jenny Lind is, perhaps, the most commemorated of all stage figures. There are two Jenny Lind transfers recorded, both of which include a nightingale and which appear on a wide variety of ware. There is also a gin flask of a lady holding a bird which is often, and probably correctly, ascribed to Jenny Lind. All Jenny Lind commemoratives were almost certainly made in 1847, when she made her début in London and a positive Jenny Lind fever swept the land.

20. A very rare transfer featuring Fanny Kemble in the role of Belvidera, a part she first played in December 1829.

21. There have been a considerable number of famous thespian elephants: this particular one appeared in a play called *The Elephant of Siam* at the Adelphi Theatre in 1829. He is also featured as a number of Staffordshire figures.

22. A very rare sporting commemorative indeed, the transfer recorded only on this particular plate. 'Colonel' belonged originally to the Hon. Edward Petre, and won perpetual fame by dead-heating the 1828 Derby. He was sold to George IV that same year, but proved a royal disappointment and was, a few years later, 'exported to Germany'. Another commemorated race-horse is Foigh-a-Ballagh, winner of the 1844 St Leger.

The second leg of the transport revolution, the major development of road travel, came somewhat later, and subdivided into two separate but apposite aspects: a marked improvement to the roads: a radical change in the vehicles that crossed them.

The latter began in 1785, when John Palmer started his first mail coach service from Bristol to London. A year later he was appointed Controller General of the Post Office, and the mail coach began to span the country with the first really rapid and reliable hard-surface travel and news-delivery service.

All of which greatly encouraged that combined dissemination of news and goods which formed the basis of an ever increasingly flourishing commemorative era.

But as much responsible for this as the improvement in vehicular design construction and organization was the marked improvement in road engineering.

This began with the concept of turn-pike trusts. These were speculative financial arrangements by which stretches of road were hired out on a toll basis to syndicates of investors who in return undertook to maintain them, thus, happily, removing the onus of road repairs from the largely ineffectual village councils and producing at least short 'reaches' of fast,

23. Children's plates commemorating the opening of the tunnel under the Thames between Rotherhithe and Wapping are to be found transferred in both black and red. The tunnel, which was opened after a great many vicissitudes on March the 25th 1843 was the brainchild of Sir Mark Brunel (see plate 6). There is also a very rare salt-glaze gin flask marking this event

effective surface.

By the beginning of the nineteenth century the efforts of these turnpikers were supported by considerable technical advances: as early as 1824 the term 'Macadamizing' had passed into the English language.

The success of the 'pike' increase can be judged by the fact that at its peak, in 1837, there were 1,100 separate trusts, responsible for the upkeep of some 22,000 miles of road.

Last in this trilogy of transport development came the railways. On September the 15th 1830 the Duke of Wellington opened the Manchester/Liverpool line and the railway age had truly begun.

The first great railway boom stretched from 1830 to 1840. During that time 1,497 miles of railway were built, in contrast to the 97 miles that had existed in 1830.

There then came some slight cessation, followed by the incredible railway mania of 1845 when nearly 5,000 miles were authorized by Parliament. This fever lasted until the sudden collapse of public confidence, and the subsequent scandal of George Hudson's financial finaglings, which left a trail of ruined small investors behind it, and this in turn

24. Boxing and boxers were enthusiastically commemorated in the late 18th and early 19th century. This particular transfer, which was created by that very meticulous engraver Aynsely of Lane End, shows Humphreys and Mendoza during their fight at Odiham in Hampshire in 1788.
Other recorded boxers include Ben Caunt, Tom Johnson, Isaac Perrins, Tom Spring, Jack Langan and, most commonly of all, Molyneux and Cribb.

MANCHESTER SHIP CANAL

PLATT'S YACHT "NORSEMAN," IN 80-FOOT LOCK, EAST

5. Both the start and the completion of the Manchester Ship Canal were celebrated with commemorative pottery. The former produced a plate featuring the ox-roast held to celebrate the passing of the parliamentary bill, the latter was honoured by a wide variety of pieces and of transfers. Many feature Daniel Adamson, the progenitor of the scheme and chairman of the company at its inauguration. The particular transfer is rare: who 'Mr Platt' was is not yet known.

was the precursor of a decade of solid development. By 1860 virtually all the main lines had been built and Britain was, to all intents and purposes, as potentially mobile as she is today.

Fourthly, and arising directly from this huge improvement in communications, there was a startling change in the amount of information the populace at large had about the affairs of the day.

Prior to the mail coaches the postal service had been, to say the least of it, rudimentary in the extreme.

By the end of the eighteenth century a marked improvement had been made in speed and efficiency, but the cost was still too high for the labouring classes greatly to benefit from the change.

However, from the turn of the century on, with the immense improvements in roads and the final achievements of the railways, costs fell steadily. Finally, of course, in the 1840s, Rowland Hill's penny post brought a frequent exchange of news within the reach of all but the unemployed.

Newspapers, too, greatly increased their circulation: *The Times*, in 1794 had a circulation of only 2,000. In 1836 this had risen to 10,000 and by 1860 was 53,000.

And these years saw the spread of a very significant provincial press.

The reasons for this were not all, of course, appertaining to better distribution facilities. There was also, in the period, a marked increase in education and literacy, and a marked participation in an interest in current affairs by the newly emergent lower-middle, artisan, class. This saw, perhaps, its greatest advance from 1823 on, when Dr Birkbeck's concept of Mechanics' Institutes, taken up and given impetus by Henry Brougham, swept through the land. In 1824 the *Mechanics' Magazine* sold 16,000 copies, and 1,500 workmen subscribed a guinea apiece to the London Institute alone.

This new phenomenon of a semi-educated artisan class meant that now almost everybody in Britain had at the very least access to someone who knew someone who could read and so disseminate the news and views of the moment. No longer was the country subject to the confident censorship of the Squirearchy, who, secure in the knowledge that no one could give them the lie, had tended to release only the news.

26. Fred Archer is probably still the most famous jockey ever to have ridden in Britain. His tragic death in 1886 (he committed suicide) was commemorated by one of the octagonal plates which make up such an interesting part of late-19th-century collecting.

they considered 'good' for the people.

The result was, inevitably, a far greater use of pottery both as a persuasive medium (e.g. the large number of election bowls and tankards distributed by Bell in his 1826 campaign in Northumberland and the mass of ware issued round and about the 1832 Reform Bill) and as a celebratory souvenir (e.g. the immense number of Coronation pieces published for the Coronation of William IV in the considerable national enthusiasm at seeing the last of George IV!).

Fifth, and lastly, there was a marked leap in population and, because of the increase in industry and the plethora of enclosures, such a concentration into large manufacturing townships, that the census of 1851 shows a full half of the total population living an urban existence.

So in the period 1780 to 1850 Britain changed from a small, largely uneducated, rural populace living isolated lives in highly parochial circumstances to a rapidly growing, at least partially educated urban populace, living intensely socially conscious lives in extremely nationalistic circumstances.

And this transformation, coupled with the great technical advances already discussed, resulted in the very considerable demand for, and supply of, commemorative pottery that the one hundred and twenty years with which this book concerns itself so fruitfully produced.

27. Pieces commemorating strikes or lock-outs and their resultant problems were quite a minor feature of the later 19th century. A particularly dramatic series of transfers, for instance, was produced to commemorate the Blackburn riots in 1878. This particular plate celebrates the 1871 struggle of the Tyneside workers for a nine-hour day; Burnett, the bearded central figure, was the president of the 'Nine Hour League'.

28. This mug, black-printed with, amongst other designs, the verse

  "Britons rejoyce cheer up and sing,
   And drink this health, Long live the King,"

was published in 1789: the couplet appears on a wide variety of ware.

In 1780 George III was on the throne, Lord North was Prime Minister, and Britain had been at war with the American Colonies for five years.

It was not a popular war. And possibly because it was not a popular war and George was not a popular King there is, at the start of this commemorative span, no recorded royal piece produced. The first, in fact, comes in 1789 with the attack of Royal Madness.

In October 1788 King George contracted a bad chill of the stomach and bowels. By November his condition had deteriorated sufficiently to precipitate a major political crisis.

The King was a fervent supporter of Pitt and the Tories.

The Prince of Wales was an equally fervent supporter of Fox and the Opposition.

Both parties immediately began a fierce campaign both in and out of the House: Pitt to forestall any attempt to introduce a Regency Bill, for this would surely have meant his dismissal from office; Fox and the Whigs to promote one in the certainty that they would immediately become, through Royal Patronage, the party in power.

The Tories, then and up to March 1789 when the King was judged to be fully recovered, issued a number of pieces advocating health to the King. These usually show the head of George III and the rhyme "Britons Rejoice, Cheer up and Sing and drink this Health, God Save the King."

There is one transfer, appearing on a creamware mug, which shows a small bust profile portrait of George III flanked by the lion and unicorn, flags, battle emblems, and the cap of liberty, and including in the design the royal coat of arms, around which is the inscription "The Fountain of Honour Mar. 17. 1789", with above the words "God Save the King" and beneath, the rhyming couplet quoted. (The St Paul's service of Thanksgiving for the royal recovery, incidentally, had taken place on March the 15th.)

There were, however, variations. Another transfer shows Britannia and lion with a portrait of George III above the verses:

"Indulgent mercy from th' Almighty Throne
O'er regal grief benignant shone
To transport turn'd a people's fears
And stayed a people's tide of tears
And gave a Sovereign o'er a joyful land,
    Again with vigorous grasp to stretch ye sceptr'd
    hand."

And various bowls simply painted "The King" were almost certainly made at this time.

Some of these transfers, however, were re-used for the jubilee in 1809: the collector must judge from the condition of the pottery and style of the ancillary decoration, if any, whether it is a late eighteenth century or an early nineteenth century piece.

One interesting result of the bout of Royal Madness was the abrupt end of Prince William Henry's naval career. Summoned back to the royal invalid, he arrived in April 1789 and unwisely let his father see that his sympathies lay with the Whigs. For punishment he was created Duke of Clarence and, apart from fifteen months in 1827–8 when he was made Lord High Admiral, debarred from ever having any further connection with the service for which he showed such keenness.

Ironically, in that year, and presumably as part of the general enthusiasm for the Royal Family that accompanied the King's recovery, a very rare jug applauding Prince William's naval career was published. This is 23.75cm high, creamware with black transferring, and is dated 1789. On the one side it shows a bust portrait of the young Prince in naval uniform, with underneath the clerihew "He's Royal, he's noble, he's chosen to be, the Guard of our Island and Prince of the Sea." On the reverse is a spirited scene of naval battle, possibly intended to represent Rodney's relief of Gibraltar. The jug was almost certainly both potted and printed in Liverpool.

29. A very rare jug indeed. One example has been seen marked Wedgewood & Co. This dates it pretty precisely between 1785 when the factory started and 1789 when Prince William Henry became Duke of Clarence, which supports the authenticity of the unmarked jug dated 1789.

20. A miniature spirit flask almost certainly made in or about 1793. By courtesy of the Museum and Art Gallery, Warrington.

21. With the wording "KING and CONSTITUTION", such a piece was almost certainly made around 1793, at the outbreak of war with France. Without this anti-Jacobin slogan it would more probably be made for the Golden Jubilee in 1809/10.

While the madness of King George had been occurring, the French had been busy revolting and, in January 1793, executing their King. Directly arising from this, in February, France, already at war with the Austrian/Prussian Coalition and Spain and now attacking Holland, declared war on England.

Britain immediately mustered a force of ten thousand soldiers and dispatched them under the command of the Duke of York (George III's second son) to serve under the Prince of Coburg. The Duke was than a lieutenant-general, a rank he had attained on 27 October 1789. At first the allies were extremely successful, sweeping the French from Belgium and on the 26th of July taking the stubbornly defended town of Valenciennes.

A considerable number of pieces were published during this period, many specifically celebrating the Duke of York's success at Valenciennes. The most common transfer shows the Duke directing the battle, and is encaptioned "The Duke of York at Valenciennes". It is a print to beware of; the authors have seen it on jugs that were certainly made in the early nineteenth century, and it is undoubtedly one of those

18

cases where a most careful scrutiny of the actual pot must determine whether the piece is genuinely commemorative or whether it has simply been used for general decoration. The figure of the Duke of York on horseback, which is seen in contemporary Valenciennes transfers, also appears in transfers and mouldings up to the early nineteenth century, and indeed there are some very suspect mid-nineteenth-century moulded pieces which show the same figure.

There are however four prints which the authors at least have never seen used as general decoration:

1. A castle under heavy attack with a small group of British staff officers in the foreground, the print encaptioned "Storming and taking Valenciennes by the British Troops &c Under the Command of His Royal Highness the Duke of York".

2. A most elaborate view of the British tented camp with a spirited mortar attack on the fortress in the distance, and in extreme close-up, H.R.H. with sword drawn and horse a-prance, encaptioned "His Royal Highness Frederick Duke of York".

3. The Duke at Valenciennes, featuring the mortars being fired, with detailed dotted outline of the trajectories of the projectiles.

4. A kneeling French officer surrendering the keys of the fortress to a British general. In a surrounding cartouche are the captions "Surrender of Valenciennes" and "Gen/l Ferand delivering the keys to His Royal Highness the Duke of York".

There is also a particularly striking picture of the mounted Duke, black printed on a fine 16.25cm high creamware jug, and dated 1795 – possibly commemorating his promotion to field marshal on February the 11th.

However, many of the early portrait pieces, simply captioned "The Duke of York" are probably more a general expression of loyal enthusiasm than commemorative of a particular event. Into this category falls a splendid creamware teapot bearing a moulded bust portrait encaptioned "Frederick Duke of York", with on the reverse a rare portrait of his brother George, as a wispy-haired young prince, encaptioned "George Prince of Wales". Both portraits are very

32. One of the many transfers made to celebrate the Duke of York's success at Valenciennes. This transfer is almost certainly confined to contemporary pieces. By courtesy of the City of Liverpool Museums.

33. On the reverse of this Valenciennes jug is a very rare print of General O'Hara just before being taken prisoner by the French on November the 30th 1793.

24. A very beautiful Pratt palette plate, probably made in Liverpool.

finely moulded and overglaze polychrome painted.

Another favourite of this period is a range of Pratt flasks, jugs and tankards, moulded and painted underglaze in high temperature colours, showing on the one side a bust portrait group of Louis XVI, his wife and son and on the other a bust portrait figure of the Duke of York, which were almost certainly originally published in 1793, when the army was expected to sweep to victory and to avenge the French Royal Family.

There does not seem to have been anything published specifically to commemorate Britain's entry into the war. But there are a number of royal transfer which may very well have been produced at this time. These are fully dealt with in the section on Naval and Military People and Events.

And so, at war with France, Britain passed into the nineteenth century. For obvious reasons the Royal Family and their doings now took second place, first to the admirals, particularly Nelson, and their great victories and then, a

25. The trajectories of the mortar bombs aimed at Valenciennes are clearly defined by the dotted lines.

20

little later, to the meteoric campaigns and career of Wellington. In fact from the late 1790s until the end of the war in 1814 little royal ware appears to have been made.

There were, however, noted exceptions.

In September 1806 the Prince of Wales and the Duke of Clarence when stopping at Trentham Hall, visited the Stoke Potteries. The *Staffordshire Advertiser* of September the 20th 1806 reports:

> On the Friday morning their Royal Highnesses proceeded to Stoke-upon-Trent and immediately visited the extensive manufactory of Mr. Spode . . . as a mark of his approbation the Prince of Wales was graciously pleased to allow Mr. Spode the distinguishing privilege of considering himself 'Potter of English porcelain, Manufacturer to His Royal Highness'.

To commemorate this visit a flask was produced, probably by the Spode pottery, which, after all, had most to commemorate. It is of pearlware 15.00cm high, decorated under the glaze with high-temperature colours – yellow, brown and blue. The basic colour of the flask is yellow, with freely painted brown decoration, but in the centre of each side is a

37. An old print revived: without the anti-Jacobin sentiments this is almost certainly an 1809 piece. These tankards are often printed in black, with blue decoration round the rim, and may have been made in Swansea.

bold blue panel with the Prince of Wales' Feathers painted in brown inside a decoration of brown bands.

Then in 1809 the country celebrated the official jubilee of the King; jubilee year, "The Grand National Jubilee" as it was called, actually starting on October the 25th.

Curiously, although George was after all the first English king since Edward III to achieve a full fifty years' reign, there were few variations of transfers published to celebrate this event. The most interesting is on a series of very similar creamware jugs, black printed and potted at the Herculaneum pottery in Liverpool. The transfers vary slightly but in general feature a large and elaborate coat of arms, with the Hanoverian inescutcheon, signed 'Dixon' and dated 1803, and the Liverpool 'Amnesty' print. This consists of the Spirit of History and of Britannia, standing amidst clouds, and supporting a scroll emblazoned "Happy would England be, Could George but live to see, Another JUBILEE", with a cypher of "G III R 50" above. The whole being set above a scene of a prison or castle (unidentified) flying the Union Jack and standing beside an equestrian statue of George III in Roman dress, on the plinth of which is a clearly defined liver bird. From the 'prison' a considerable number of people are hurrying forth. The print is encaptioned: "Let the prisoners go free. Give GOD praise Jubilee 25th October 1809."

This monument – without, in fact, the liver bird – was erected by public subscription to mark the jubilee and is still standing in Liverpool at the junction of Pembroke Place and London Road. The terms of the jubilee amnesty, apparently, were:

1. Pardon for deserters – Naval deserters absolutely but Army deserters required to rejoin.
2. Pardon for all armed forces offences.
3. A subscription raised to discharge insolvent debtors.
4. An amnesty for all P.O.Ws except the French

There was not however, despite the fine wording of the caption, any pardon at all for ordinary criminals.

The only other known transfer which can absolutely be said to commemorate the jubilee is to be seen on another creamware jug, 20.00 cm high, again potted and printed in

22

Two very fine plaques: the one is possibly the only contemporary piece to regret the death of Fox, the other stems from Alfred Crowquill's figure of Wellington

Liverpool. The black transfer shows a portrait of George III facing three-quarters to front. The portrait is in an oval medallion, with the crown at the top, and the emblems of War, Religion and Justice at the base. Beneath is the inscription "George the Third in the 51st year of his Reign".

But there are several less-detailed transfers which were almost certainly published, or republished, for the jubilee. Most of them show the King and Queen in bust profile in classic style, with the words "A King Rever'd, a Queen Belov'd". Another frequent combination is a profile portrait of George III, with the famous Dixon coat of arms described above.

The next royal event to be ceramically commemorated was a remarkably trivial one. On January the 14th 1813 Lady Charlotte Campbell, the Princess of Wales's lady-in-waiting, handed to the Lords Liverpool and Eldon a letter to the Regent. The next day it returned. Unopened. On the 16th it went back to the noble lords. Again it returned, unopened. On the 17th it was back with the lords again, and this time the contents were said to have been made known to the Regent. But no answer was vouchsafed. And so Caroline, or so it was claimed, published the letter. Anyway, it was published. And revealed to be a fervent plea to see more of the Princess Charlotte, her only child, who had been removed to Windsor. But the publication of this letter had precisely the opposite effect. Charlotte came to London and was promised to visit her mother on February the 11th; but on that very morning Caroline received not the Princess but a curt information that she was refused coming. Not unnaturally she asked why. And on February the 14th, St Valentine's day, Lord Liverpool replied that it was "in consequence of the publication, in the *Morning Chronicle* of the 10th instant of a letter addressed by your Royal Highness to the Prince Regent". And there the correspondence ended. But the populace enjoyed it while it lasted and there was one jug published to record this absurd exchange of *billets-doux*. It features a satirical transfer encaptioned "Regent Valentine" and shows the Regent, with plume of feathers and two serpents twined about him, with behind him a stern Britannia and lion (equally stern) and a kneeling woman (Caroline?)

38. Surely one of the most absurd Royal events ever commemorated: the *dramatis personae* are, presumably, Charlotte, Caroline and George.

23

39. These moulded jugs come in a range
of sizes, and all have lustre decoration.
They are what one might call the 'classic'
Charlotte/Leopold marriage souvenir

holding out a letter addressed "To the Prince Regent". In front of the Regent and a little in the background is another female, wearing a plume of feathers (Charlotte?) watching the scene.

Three years later, on May the 2nd 1816, England's hope, the Princess Charlotte, Princess of Wales, married Prince Leopold of Saxe-Coburg.

Poor Charlotte had led a disturbed life. An early victim of the continuing squabble between her father and mother, she had first, in 1814, been betrothed to the Prince of Orange. This event was celebrated by the issue of at least one very decorative piece: a beautifully potted creamware plate, printed with an orange tree and the legend "Orange Boven" (Long Live the House of Orange), probably made in Sunderland and probably exported to a country more enthusiastic about the match than either the British or the Princess, who had meanwhile become infatuated with Prince Augustus of Prussia.

The match fell through. And in 1815 she wrote, Augustus having been firmly declared impossible, "I have decidedly fixed on Prince Leopold." (The Prince had first come over in

24

the summer of 1814, in the suite of the Emperor Alexander, and had been presented to Charlotte then.) In January 1816 Castlereagh wrote telling Leopold that the Regent had agreed to the marriage and in February the young Prince came over to Brighton.

They were married at Carlton House on May the 2nd.

It was quite a wedding. The service began a little after nine o'clock and took place in the Grand Crimson Saloon of Carlton House, with the Archbishop of Canterbury officiating, the Bishop of Wales assisting and the Prince Regent, resplendent in a scarlet field marshal's coat, giving away the bride. Charlotte wore a dress of silver lamé on net, trimmed with Brussels lace, with a headdress, of rosebuds and leaves, composed of the most superb brilliants (this she is often shown wearing on transfers commemorating her death). Leopold wore "a British General's full uniform, white kerstymere waistcoat and small clothes, with a magnificent sword and costly belt, adorned with diamonds and various other priceless gems". He also wore all his decorations (again this costume is to be seen on 1817 commemorative pieces).

The most popular pieces published to record this happy event were a series of moulded jugs. They are lavishly decorated with lustre and have raised, moulded bust portraits of the Prince on the one side and of the Princess on the other. Both are looking to dexter: he is wearing civilian clothes and she is wearing the headdress with three roses in it which she wore at the wedding; she also wears two rows of beads (although in the illustration in *La Belle Assemblée* of July 1816 she is shown with a one-strand necklace). The figures themselves are normally decorated with lustre, but on occasions they are to be seen overglaze enamelled in a particularly brilliant palette. The handle of the jug is a simple scroll. The jugs are undoubtedly Staffordshire in origin, but could have come from any factory.

Charlotte's marriage would appear to have been a happy one. They settled at Claremont, a fine house in Esher given them by the Regent, and, by the spring of 1817, she was pregnant.

There are two plates, both marked 'A. Stevenson, Warranted Staffordshire', and both published after her death,

40. This print appears on various plates and saucer dishes, but this is the only version to carry a caption. The original picture of Charlotte, Leopold and Goody Bewley is in Green's book.

which portray this period of the Princess's life.

The one shows simply a transfer view of Claremont House, painted in Pratt palette, with the inscription "The Grand Front of Claremont House. The Seat of her late Royal Highness Princess Charlotte and Prince Leopold."

The second concerns that curious old crone Goody Bewley and her Bible.

In the grounds of Claremont there was a small cottage, in which had lived for seventeen years an old woman named Mary Bewley, often called Goody Bewley. This old lady was frequently visited by Prince Leopold and Princess Charlotte. Thomas Green, who wrote one of the more believable histories of Charlotte, describes the Bible incident:

In the autumn of 1816, when walking with Prince Leopold, the Princess Charlotte saw Goody Bewley sitting at the cottage door reading a book, and asked her what she was

26

41. One of the many variants of transfer made to lament the death of Charlotte in 1817. They are most often found printed on rather inferior porcelainous tea-sets.

reading. She replied 'Please, my Princess, a book that I am very fond of'. It was an old small-print Bible. The Princess looked at it, and said 'The print is too small for you: but if you love reading, I have a book I will give you'. About a month afterwards, one cold wet evening in December, Her Royal Highness and Prince Leopold came again on foot, followed by a single domestic carrying a large beautifully bound quarto Bible; The Princess herself brought a Prayer Book and gave both it and the Bible to the old woman.

An adaptation of a print in Green's book showing the royal couple with the old woman appears on the second plate, which is also decorated in Pratt palette and carries the inscription: "Princess Charlotte and Prince Leopold Finding Dame Bewley at her Cottage Door reading her old Bible".

One other piece, also published after Charlotte's death,

recalls the couple at Claremont. This is a blue-and-white printed plate showing the Prince and Princess in the grounds, with Claremont House in the background, speaking to a kneeling woman and child. Behind them is a single groom, holding the Prince's horse and the Princess's pony chaise – their recorded forms of transport about the estate during the Princess's pregnancy. This plate has no caption, and is marked on the base simply "British Views", but the scene marries up to a fairly detailed description in Green's book.

It was at Claremont, on November the 3rd 1817, that Princess Charlotte's labour pains began; where, on November the 5th she was delivered of a stillborn son, and where, at 2.30 a.m. on the 6th, she died.

It was a major national tragedy, and a prodigious quantity of ware was made to commemorate the event.

Chief amongst these were complete tea services of porcellainous ware – either black-rimmed or pink-lustre-trimmed. They carried a vast selection of differing but very similar transfers featuring either Charlotte or her tomb or Leopold

42. An extremely rare Charlotte memorial plate.

43. A very rare creamware tankard, brown-printed, deriding the engagement of Charlotte and of Leopold: £30,000 was the maiden Princess's civil list allocation.

44. A very unusual version of the death of Charlotte.

45. This Charlotte transfer is usually found on very finely potted children's plates, sometimes further decorated with brown rims.

46. Another variant on the tea-set motifs lamenting the death of Charlotte.

46. Another variant on the tea-set motifs lamenting the death of Charlotte.

or a mourning Britannia or all or any in varied combinations.

As well as these, which on the whole are neither very well potted nor printed, there is a very fine transfer of a semi-profile of Charlotte in her wedding headdress and inscribed in plain capitals and elaborate script "In commemoration of THE LATE AND MUCH LAMENTED Princess Charlotte of Saxe Coburg who departed this life November 6th 1817." This usually appears on creamware children's plates with very finely moulded floral borders, but has also been seen, coupled with a profile of Leopold in the military uniform he wore at the wedding and inscribed in plain capitals "PRINCE LEOPOLD", on very well potted spill vases, and on a very rare pair of porcelainous plaques.

In the years following 1817 royal death followed royal death: on November the 17th 1818 Queen Charlotte died; on January the 23rd 1820 the Duke of Kent (Victoria's father) died; on January the 29th King George III died.

There would appear to be nothing published in pottery to commemorate the death of Queen Charlotte.

30

47. The death of the Duke of Kent (Victoria's father) was most often lamented by well-potted children's plates carrying this transfer. A very slightly different transfer appears on spill vases.

For the Duke of Kent there is only one known commemorative transfer, almost certainly published at his death – a simple bust portrait of the Duke in military uniform encaptioned "The Duke of Kent". This is a rare print and has been seen only on children's plates and, with a small variation, on spill vases. In both cases it is black-printed on good quality pot.

Transfers of the death of George III are also hard to come by. The only one which the authors know and which is specifically commemorative shows a bust profile portrait of George III in uniform, with the inscription "Sacred to the Memory of George III who died 29 Jan 1820". This transfer appears in blue on a very finely potted children's plate with moulded floral border; and also (without inscription) in the central medallion of a boldly printed blue-and-white plate, 25.00 cm in diameter, with a transferred border of Royal Flowers.

It is interesting to note that similar blue-and-white plates appear with different medallion centres: there is one with Queen Caroline, unnamed, but identified from contemporary

48. 49. Both sides of a very rare jug, possibly celebrating the marriage of Charlotte and Leopold, but more probably lamenting her death. The Charlotte print has also been seen encaptioned for Queen Caroline. (See plate 53.)

50. This print, lamenting the death of George III, appears on children's plates both blue-printed and, more rarely, in Pratt palette. It also occurs as one of the centre medallion motifs of a blue-and-white dinner service. The quotation clearly links it to the Lancasterian School movement. (See plate 51.)

prints; there is another showing a small child receiving a book from George III. These bold blue-and-white designs, although far from plentiful, have been seen on soup plates as well as dinner plates, and would indicate that perhaps a whole dinner service, with varying individual central medallion transfers, was made.

The transfer of the kneeling child receiving a book from George III also appears on children's plates with the caption "I hope the time will come when every poor child in my dominions will be able to read the bible". These have been seen either blue-printed, or (more rarely) most beautifully decorated in a Pratt palette.

This print was almost certainly associated with the work of the Lancasterian Schools for the children of the poor, of which the King was a patron. Joseph Lancaster perfected the monitorial system; he teaching the monitors, the monitors teaching the rest of the group. By 1804 he had some five hundred pupils and his school was famous. By 1807 there were forty-five schools and Lancaster was in prison for debt. From this he was rescued by Joseph Fox, who formed a governing

33

51. This blue-and-white printed dinner service carries a wide variety of motifs including this one regretting the death of George III. Others feature Queen Caroline, 'Farmer George', etc. (See plate 50.)

52. Cups and saucers commemorating the death of the Duke of York are surprisingly rare. Once he had left active service York was little commemorated. But there were a few and very rare pieces made at the time of the Mary Clarke scandal.

committee of six. The committee were scarcely more competent than Lancaster, and in 1810 they turned, *en masse*, to Brougham to sort out the mess. Brougham, at a public meeting on May the 11th 1811, established the Royal Lancasterian Institution.

When George III received Lancaster it is reported that he said to him: "It is my wish that every poor child in my kingdom may be taught to read the Bible." The text on the children's plates clearly originates from this. The plates were, presumably, published at the time of the King's death, very possibly being distributed to the pupils of the schools.

And so, on January the 31st 1820 George IV was proclaimed king, and England was about to reel under the rip-roaring royal scandal of the Bill of Pains and Penalties.

But before this the proclamation itself was honoured by matched pairs of transfers of George and Caroline. The transfers are captioned respectively "HER MOST GRACIOUS MAJESTY Queen Caroline", "GEORGE IV Born August 12th 1762 Proclaimed King of England Jan. 31st 1820" and are usually found on plaques or on children's plates.

Once George was King, Caroline, urged by the ruthless ambitions of the Whigs and in particular of Henry Brougham, left Italy, where she had lived since 1814, for France.

From Calais, accompanied by Alderman Wood, Caroline embarked on the cross-channel packet *Prince Leopold* (George having refused her the use of an official ship) and at one o'clock in the afternoon of January the 5th landed at Dover. She was wearing, according to her contemporary chronicler Robert Huish, a black sarcenet gown, white ruff, black satin hat and rich plume of black ostrich feathers. In all the myriad pieces of Carolinia published, one of the most striking features is her hats – and most of them are in fact a variation on this, the landing hat.

This scene is reproduced in transfer and appears on a jug with the mis-spelled inscription: "Queen Cariline landing at Dover".

Once landed, Caroline went to London and established herself at Wood's house in South Audley Street. From here she moved to a house in Portman Street and later, in August,

53. This same print can be seen, encaptioned as Princess Charlotte. (See plates 48/49.)

54. One of the rarer Queen Caroline pieces, these plaques are richly decorated in pink lustre. Although they are unmarked, popular attribution connects them with Swansea.

35

55. One of the 'classic' Caroline pieces, this transfer, with variants to the detailing on the hat, and various captions, appears on a wide range of plates, often printed in blue.

56. One of many rhymes supporting Caroline during the Bill of Pains and Penalties: they are often found on the reverse of jugs carrying one or other of her portraits.

MAY THE DIAMONDS IN THE BRITISH CROWN GLITTER ON THE HEAD OF OUR NOBLE QUEEN CAROLINE.

took final residence at Brandenburg House, Hammersmith.

The idea of Caroline as Queen was anathema to George IV. The idea of promoting her claims, hugely embarrassing both the King and the Tories, and finding sweet revenge for the Regent's coat-turning of 1811, was immensely attractive to the Whigs.

And so the campaigns began.

Caroline received loyal addresses, loyal proclamations, body after body of loyal citizens, and was soundly huzza'd and cheered as she drove through the streets. George retired to Brighton.

Lord Liverpool, the Tory leader, relying heavily on the evidence collected by the Milan commission (in 1818 a commission had been appointed by the Regent to go to Milan and attempt to gather sufficient evidence for a divorce) brought to parliament a Bill of Pains and Penalties, presented to the Lords on July the 5th as "An Act, entitled an Act

57. Possibly the rarest piece of Carolinea known.

37

58. The Villa d'Este was Caroline's house on lake Como: the transfer appears on plates printed in either blue or black, but has so far been recorded only on plates

for depriving Caroline Amelia Elizabeth, Queen of Great Britain, of and from the stile and title of Queen of these realms, and of and from the rights, prerogatives, and immunities now belonging to her as Queen Consort".

The whole case rested on the question of the Queen's alleged adultery with Count Bartolommeo Bergami, or Pergami as he was variously called, both at her Italian home, the Villa d'Este on Lake Como, and in sundry other places, including a much publicized *polacca* during a trip to Syracuse. The Villa d'Este is featured in a very beautiful transfer which appears on a variety of wares including a fine 25.00 cm blue-and-white plate and which shows the Villa, a substantial square building, nestling under the hills in the background with Caroline and Bergami sitting under an awning in a 6-oared boat in the foreground.

The Queen's advocates in the House were Brougham, her Attorney General, Denman, her Solicitor General, Dr Lushington, who was to become an executor of her will, and Mr Williams. All these *dramatis personae* appear in name on various commemorative pieces; together with Waithman (the Sheriff of Middlesex), and of course, the ubiquitous Alderman Wood. But the only known published portrait

38

His Royal Highnefs *FREDERICK DUKE* of YORK.

A magnificent punch bowl, 1793–4, possibly made in Swansea   Colour Plate 2

59. The most interesting detail of this print is the tiny angelic figure of Charlotte in the top left hand, encaptioned "Protect my Mother".

pieces are of Wood, who appears in applique bust portrait on a lustre jug, and of Brougham and Denman. These latter have been seen on the one moulded jug, 12.00 cm high and 9.00 cm in diameter. On the one side is a head-and-shoulders portrait of Brougham, in a panel surrounded by moulded flowers, and on the rim is the moulded caption "H Brougham Esq M.P.". On the reverse is a similar portrait of Denman in similar setting, with the caption "T. Denman Esq M.P.".

The trial, for such it really was, started on August the 17th. The Queen attended but did not participate (she is shown, in an oil painting by Sir George Hayter, now in the National Portrait Gallery, sitting at the trial wearing a lace 'mantilla': this style of headdress appears on one rather rare transfer). With breaks it continued until November the 10th.

During the trial a wide and sordid variety of witnesses were called, both English and Italian. And the most intimate details of the luckless Queen's private life were paraded in front of a fascinated House. Indeed the whole affair seems largely to have rested on the unsavoury evidence of soiled bed-sheets, used nightsoil pots, and the proximity of Caroline's room and/or bed to Bergami's. The evidence of the Milan

60. These jugs occur in a variety of sizes printed in either black or pink and, in both cases, freely decorated with lustre. The reverse carries a rhyme satirizing the "Green Bag Crew". For this reason they are often catalogued as "Green Bag" jugs.

commission was much used, and incidentally, brought to the House in a green baize bag. Slighting references to this green bag appear on plates and jugs.

The Lords, just, decided against her. And the bill was carried on October the 24th, but by a majority of only twenty-eight.

Nevertheless the King and the Government insisted that it go to committee. The committee duly sat, considered, and reported to the House on November the 9th. Lord Liverpool "saw clearly that the bill was doomed" but "the Chancellor (Eldon) characteristically resisted the proposal of abandonment". The next day, duly, Lord Eldon tried for a third reading. But when the majority for this dwindled to nine even the hoariest Tory knew defeat when he saw it.

And the bill was withdrawn.

The people were triumphant.

In fact they had little to congratulate themselves on. There was little doubt that Caroline was a nymphomaniac who had certainly committed adultery with Bergami – and many others. On the other hand George IV's lack of morals was notorious, and to add to the general lack of charm surrounding his peccadillos, it is well to remember that all his mistresses were older than he, and that Lady Conyngham, when she became his last love, was already a grandmother.

All in all, George and Caroline seem to have deserved each other!

However, Caroline's return to England and the 'trial' provided ammunition for a huge quantity of commemorative pottery, most of which features varying portraits of Caroline in one or other of her splendid hats, supported by a selection of delightful poems scanned to be sung either to the National Anthem or to popular tunes of the day. A typical example and, perhaps, the most commonly seen is a very finely potted jug. This has a deep-pink-lustre trim, with on the one side a print of Caroline in a flat, squashed-down hat trimmed with two feathers on its right-hand side (she is sporting a rather similar hat, but without the feathers, in a print issued in 1820 showing her entry into Jerusalem, which she visited with Bergami in 1816), wearing a ruffed dress and a double string of pearls from which hangs a pendant, the print

encaptioned – in shadowed lettering – "GOD SAVE QUEEN CAROLINE!", and on the other in a leaf and ribbon cartouche the words (at the top) "LONG LIVE QUEEN CAROLINE" (and at the bottom) "QUEEN OF ENGLAND"; completing the circle of the cartouche are the names of her supporters – Brougham, Wood, Lushington, Denman, Waithman, Williams. The royal crown is above all, the Royal Flowers below all. In the centre of the cartouche is this parody of the National Anthem:—

> As for the Green Bag crew,
> Justice will have it due,
> God save the Queen!
> Confound this politicks,
> Frustrate this knavish tricks,
> On HER our hopes we fix,
> God save the Queen.

Other verses and portrait appearing in different combina-

41

62. This print sometimes occurs without its caption. This particular spill vase carries, perhaps, the best example of the 'Royal Wanderer' yet recorded. By courtesy of the Harris Museum and Art Gallery Preston.

63. A very rare brown salt-glaze gin flask. With the slogan on the scroll "My hope is in my People" it *must*, presumably, be Caroline.

tions or separately are:

1. Portraits:

(a) Transfers of Caroline sometimes in profile, sometimes full front, wearing the feathered 'top hat', and usually sporting a ruffle. The same appears in several moulded versions, and on both a pink lustred plaque and a pink lustre mug the moulded feathers are surmounted by the crown and on occasions by the bold initials Q.C. On some the feathers go backwards; on others there is one feather forward, one back; on others all feathers are flopping forwards. But they would all appear to be variations of the same hat.

(b) Caroline, full front bust portrait, wearing the squashy beret-type hat, again with feathers, usually associated with the green-bag rhyme, but also appearing in a medallion surrounded by the Royal Flowers in which is the enchanting admonition "Protect my Mother" – presumably coming from Princess Charlotte in Heaven above.

(c) A young Caroline, hair on top of her head, unusually pretty, with low-cut dress, necklace, the whole in a panel surmounted by the crown, with the inscription, "Her Majesty Queen Caroline". This head-and-shoulders portrait with Caroline looking to dexter has been seen only on a jug 15.00 cm high.

(d) A curly-haired Caroline in softly draped dress, with pendant and cross, and the inscription behind her, "Her Majesty Queen Caroline of England". (This exact transfer appears encaptioned 'Princess Charlotte', on a jug which also bears the portrait of Prince Leopold.)

(e) Caroline in bust portrait, wearing her lace mantilla.

(f) A young and very pretty Caroline, wearing a curiously spiky coronet, with her hair piled high on her head. Encircling this bust portrait is the inscription – "Queen Caroline or the Royal Wanderer, born May 17th 1768". This transfer has been seen only on two small creamware pieces, a spill vase and a coffee can.

2. Verses:

(a)   "May the Diamond in
         The British Crown Glitter
         On the Head of Our

Noble Queen Caroline."

(b) "May the rose of England never blow
May the thistle of Scotland never grow
May the Harp of Ireland never play
Till Queen Caroline has won the day."

(c) "I'll Sing a Song of Sixpence
A Greenbag full of lies
Four and twenty witnesses
All proved to be spies
When the bag was open'd
The Lords began to stare
To see their precious evidence
All vanished into air".

(d) "May Royal George and Caroline
Agree to rule our Nation
And Peace and Happiness combine
In every rank and station."

(e) "Would you wish to know a bright star of the morn
That cheers a whole nation all lost and forlorn
'Tis that feminine planet! O long may she shine
And Heaven protect her Our Queen Caroline.

64. These plates, with their moulded inscription 'King George IIII', are presumed to have been made at the time of the Coronation. They are often attributed to the Portobello factory, Edinburgh.

Perhaps the rarest of all Carolinian transfers is a cartoon which shows John Bull, with Caroline on one side of a scales and George on the other, weighing them one against the other. George is too light and not even the addition of sandbags, labelled "Green Bag" "Grape Shot" "Secrets" and "Spies", can help him weigh as much as Caroline. John Bull is saying: "Well done Caroline, they think to make light of you, but it won't do. I'll see fair play." George's supporters can only say "Confound that Bull, what a row he makes". This transfer has been seen only twice, on a mug and a jug.

There is also a delightful anti-George child's plate, with finely moulded flower border, and black transfer, overglaze enamelled, showing 'Prinny' and Mrs Fitzherbert on a hobby horse encaptioned "A Visit from Richmond to Carlton House". (Mrs Fitzherbert's address was No 1 Richmond Hill, but although many would like to date this plate earlier, it must have been made at the time of the Bill, for the hobby horse was not introduced into England until 1819).

Once the 'trial' was over, George IV had no reason to

postpone his coronation, and this was duly fixed for July the 19th 1821. Not unnaturally, Caroline claimed she had a right to be crowned, which claim the Privy Council immediately disallowed. But, poor woman, Caroline would not accept defeat. On the morning of Coronation Day, accompanied by Lord Hood, she sought admittance to the Abbey. . . . And was ignominiously refused. Eleven days later, while preparing to visit Drury Lane Theatre she was 'attacked by excessive sickness of the stomach'. By the next morning she was worse, and by August the 7th she was dead.

Even dead she was treated with scant dignity, her body being shipped to Brunswick after probably the most chaotic 'funeral' procession ever held.

Oddly, after the fervour of the Bill of Pains and Penalties there is little commemorating Caroline's death. Most pieces show simply a tomb scene, giving the appropriate dates and featuring a weeping Britannia. Others may show one of the known portraits, with the simple addition of the death date. But there is one most touching verse:

" 'Tis true our Gracious Queen has di'd

65. These creamware dinner plates were made especially for the Leeds Parish Church School Coronation dinner in 1821. They are very rare indeed.

No Peace for her on Earth was giv'n
    And they on Earth a crown deny'd
    We hope she'll wear a crown in Heaven."

After the plethora of Carolinia the Coronation of George IV was scantly recorded. Despite its gargantuan splendour – he spent £243,000 on it – it seems to have met with little approval or enthusiasm from the populace.

The only known pieces of Coronation ware are:

1. An 18.75cm diameter plate, with a moulded border of flowers, the Garter star, the bishop's mitre, and the royal coat of arms, and a central moulded picture of a bishop crowning George IV – with the caption in scroll cartouche "Coronation of George the IV". The whole is overglaze enamelled in polychrome palette.

2. Mug and a tankard, both bearing a red painted crown above the inscription 'G IV R, July 19, 1821'.

3. A creamware plate, diameter 21.85cm, with a black transfer of the State Crown contained within the Royal Flowers, with on a ribbon scroll above and below the inscription "George IV Crown'd July 19th 1821". (These plates, most of them marked 'Hartley Greens and Co Leeds Pottery', are said to have been used at a Coronation Dinner by the children attending the Leeds Parish Church School, each child being allowed to take away the plate he had used.)

4. A creamware mug, height 7.5cm and diameter 7.5cm, bearing a bust portrait of George, surrounded by the inscription "George the Fourth born Augt 12 1762. Succeeded to the throne Jan 29th 1819. Crowned July 19th 1821. GOD SAVE THE KING." (Thereby ante-dating the death of George III by one year.)

5. A jug, primitively painted underglaze, with Royal Flowers surrounding the body of the jug, and with beneath the spout a small blue transfer bust portrait of George, and the inscription "George IV Crowned July 19 1821".

Once George was securely crowned he set out on a series of visits to his royal dominions.

On August the 12th 1821 he went to Ireland (he actually heard of Caroline's death in Holyhead). In September he went to Hanover.

And in August 1822 he visited Scotland, becoming the first

66. This transfer, which is extremely rare, occurs on various wares. This particular jug is very roughly potted indeed.

67. The 'classic' George IV Coronation mug. A curious detail is the incorrect date of succession: given on the mug as 1819 instead of 1820. By courtesy of the Harris Museum and Art Gallery Preston.

68. A very beautiful moulded 'child's' plate usually decorated with lustre and in a brilliant polychrome palette. These Coronation plates are very rare indeed.

69. These free-style painted creamware tankards must, the authors think, be regarded with some suspicion. Certain of the recorded examples may be contemporary creamware pieces, but decorated at a considerably later date.

70. 71. Two out of three very rare transfers regretting the death of Caroline and celebrating the Coronation of George. All are blue-printed across moulded Caroline plates; the 'missing' one shows the cortège.

PART OF THE FUNERAL PROCESSION OF CAROLINE THE INJURED & PERSECUTED QUEEN OF GREAT BRITAIN. BORN MAY 17th 1768 DIED AUGt 7th 1821.

THE POWER OF PUBLIC OPINION

reigning sovereign to do so since 1688, and the first ruling Prince of Hanover ever to do so.

Landing at Leith on August the 14th, he made during his fortnight's visit to Edinburgh a marked impression on the Scots: this partly because the visit was so painstakingly and enthusiastically stage-managed by Sir Walter Scott (Scott was the first baronet created by George IV), partly because he himself entered so wholeheartedly into the display, even to the extent of wearing full Highland costume, kilt, bonnet and pink silk tights, when he rode up Princes Street for his levee at Holyrood.

The Scottish factories certainly published a number of plaques to celebrate this unique event. These plaques, many of which were probably made by the famous Portobello

47

72. A very rare pair of plates with matching transfers of George and of Caroline. Since the one transfer included the death of Caroline they were obviously made at her death and not, as at first glance they look, as Coronation souvenirs.

73. The death of Caroline was not, comparatively, lavishly commemorated. This, is perhaps the most common of the transfers. Other variants are almost indistinguishable.

48

factory, while under the management of Thomas Rathbone & Co., include one, 18.75cm by 15.00cm, with a moulded portrait of George, usually captioned in moulding "Visit of George IV to Scotland, 1822" in a surround of Scottish and Royal Flowers. It is decorated in underglaze Pratt colours, and overglaze decorated as well. There is also one rather remarkable bowl made for this event. It is only 12.5cm diameter, made of rather coarse pot and roughly painted with a primitive crown flanked by the Royal Flowers and with, under the crown, the single word "Welcome".

The next two commemorated events were royal deaths.

On January the 5th 1827 the Duke of York died at his home in Arlington House. The event is most often commemorated by a transfer, appearing on a variety of pieces, which shows a sorrowing soldier by a tomb bearing the inscription "In Memory of H.R.H. Frederick Duke of York K.G." But there is also known to exist a black transferred plate, 16.25cm diameter, with a bust portrait encaptioned "Frederick Duke of York. Born August 16 1763. Died January 5 1827".

75. The most usual piece made to regret (if that's the word) the death of George IV. The transfer appears both in black and in brown. The jugs are often marked GBH for Goodwins, Bridgwood & Harris. The reverse side carries a portrait of the late King.

76. A puzzle piece: on the bottom of the mug is a moulded inscription for the penultimate anniversary of George IV's Coronation. The authors believe the mugs may have been made for a dinner held by the Honourable Artillery Company; but this is only a theory.

Three years later, on June the 26th 1830, George IV died. His passing was little regretted ('certainly nobody was less regretted than the late King', said Greville) and little commemorated. However, one jug seen in different sizes was published by the firm of Goodwin, Bridgewood, and Harris of Lane End. It shows on the one side a portrait of a young George, and on the reverse the inscription "To the Memory of His Late Majesty King George the IV. Born August 12, 1762. Ascended the throne Jany 29 1820. Publicly proclaimed Jany 31 1820. Departed this life June 26 1830. Aged 68 years."

There is, incidentally, one puzzling piece published the year before the King's death. This is a mug dated on its base in Roman numerals 'July 19, 1829' – the anniversary of the Coronation. There was on this date a field day held by the Honourable Artillery Company and a subsequent dinner with H.R.H. the Duke of Sussex. It is possible that these mugs were produced for this. They are 9.00cm in diameter and height, with a blue background and carry a biscuit cameo of

50

George in classic style with the inscription "Georgius IV Dei Gratia Britanniarum Rex".

When William IV ascended the throne, in 1830, he was already in his sixty-fourth year and had accumulated his full share of Georgian lunatic eccentricities. Nevertheless Britain, after a surfeit of George IV, was delighted to see him.

There is, curiously, only one recorded piece commemorating his accession; a child's plate, showing in black transfer bust profile portraits of William and of Adelaide in classic style, encircled with the inscription "William IIII and Queen Adelaide Ascended the British Throne 26 June 1830". This plate also has a superb moulded border featuring busts of the King and of the Queen, flanking the State Crown.

But for his Coronation, which took place on September the 8th 1831, the number and variation of commemorative pieces published is huge and encompasses the full range of mugs, jugs, plates and plaques.

51

The transfers mostly feature various portraits of William and of Adelaide. The more commonly seen are:

(a) William in everyday clothes, and Adelaide in a morning gown, with her left hand to her face. The prints are often encaptioned "Her Most gracious Majesty Queen Adelaide" and "His most Gracious Majesty King William" and frequently occur with a transfer of the State Crown surrounded by garlands of Royal Flowers, encaptioned "King William IV and Queen Adelaide. Crowned Sep 8 1831".

(b) William in Garter robes and Adelaide in a formal gown. Both are wearing crowns. These prints are sometimes teamed with a transfer of the Garter and a Coronation date caption.

(c) Rather primitive prints of the King and Queen, William in State robes and Adelaide in a most formal gown, with a coronet on her head. The prints are not captioned.

(d) William seated on his throne, Adelaide seated, with the crown resting on a lion pillar by her left side. The prints are encaptioned "Our beloved King William 4th", "Our Amiable Queen Adelaide".

79. 80. The two sides of the most commonly seen Coronation mug: these are recorded printed in black, brown and a variety of pinks and purples.

81. An extremely unusual mug which must have been made for the Coronation since the reverse carries a transfer of the ceremony. The slipping of the transfer has produced a most curious portrait of William.

82. This is what plate 81 should look like: the impressed daisy border is very typical of children's plates of this period.

There are also several much rarer prints:

(a) A full-length picture of the King and Queen, crowned, sitting side by side on their thrones, holding orb and sceptre, the caption reading "Our Patriotic King and Queen" and giving the dates of birth of *both* of them.

(b) A bust portrait of William in 'Tudor' costume, complete with ruff, and encaptioned "His most gracious Majesty King William IV, King of Great Britain". The pair to these is a full face view of Adelaide encaptioned "Her most gracious Majesty Adelaide, Queen of Great Britain".

(c) Three picture prints, sometimes seen on Staffordshire daisy plates, sometimes on rather larger plates with borders of Swansea animals, and, very rarely, on mugs and jugs.

1. The traditional ceremony of the King's Champion riding his horse into Westminster Great Hall to throw down his gauntlet. The inscription reads "Coronation of King William the Fourth".

2. The scene in Westminster Abbey as William is crowned, encaptioned "Coronation of King William the Fourth".

3. The Coronation procession outside Westminster Abbey, again encaptioned "Coronation of King William the Fourth".

(d) An extremely rare print of an open wreath of the Royal Flowers below which is the inscription "At Westminster September 8 1831", and above which is the State Crown with above it the word "Coronation", and below it the inscription "W & A". This has been seen so far only on a pair of plates, 16.25cm diameter, with a border reminiscent of the one on the proclamation plate.

As well as these various transfer pieces there are also at least two moulded jugs. One is in copper lustre with bust figures and inscription appliqué'd in white and then enamelled, the other is marked 'Minton', and is potted in a grey dryware with very fine appliqué busts indeed.

Of all the types of ware produced jugs are far and away the most frequently found. Plates and mugs come under the more rare category.

William was a dull, elderly man who led an ordered, respectable and dull life. He always drank sparingly, ate unvaryingly (his set menu for lunch was two cutlets and two glasses of sherry) and lived in strict partnership with his plain Queen. And this, coupled with his very obvious reluctance for Reform, perhaps explains why nothing in his reign was commemorated.

Even his death on June the 20th 1837 was marked, so far as is known, by but one transfer, showing in allegoric form History and Britannia mourning at a tomb bearing the inscription "William IV Died June 20 1837. Aged 72. There is rest in Heaven".

So at five a.m. Dr Howley, the Archbishop of Canterbury, and Lord Conyngham, the Lord Chamberlain, having ridden from Windsor to Kensington, caused the young Princess Alexandrina Victoria (Victoria, before her accession was often known as the Princess 'Drina') to be woken; and the longest reign in British history had begun.

It was also the end of Britain's connection with Hanover, which enforced the Salic law. The highly unpopular Duke of Cumberland departed to become King of Hanover, and the

83. This very handsome drab-ware jug carries the Minton mark on its base. The reverse has William appliqué'd.

84. Two children's plates, probably from Staffordshire. William is shown in his Coronation robes with his curious 'Tudor' ruff (see plate 85). Adelaide is also, supposedly, in her Coronation gown.

55

85. One of a variety of scenes at the Coronation. These scenic transfers are rare.

86. One side of the 'Garter' jug. The other side has a portrait of Adelaide with a crown even more absurdly perched on her head. The front carries the garter motif and a Coronation inscription. The garter is repeated on the base of the jug.

87. Very rare indeed. These plates, which have a beautifully decorated border in polychrome palette, have been recorded printed in both black and iron-red. Curiously, the border, which presumably is intended to represent William IV, has also been seen on a plate decorated with a river scene.

88. This jug is lavishly decorated with Sunderland lustre, and brown printed with the only transfer known to record the death of William IV. An identical transfer has been seen used as a general mourning decoration, so obviously it was not engraved as a special 'Royal' plate.

89. One of the rarer young Victoria transfers. These proclamation plates are usually printed in blue.

Hanoverian inescutcheon vanished from our royal coat of arms (a useful aid to judging the age of any piece it appears on).

The stock of royalty was not marvellously high at the time for the Georgian age had, largely, been a progression from bad to worse.

It is therefore perhaps not so surprising that little was published to commemorate Victoria's accession: and on what little was, the potters made some curiously glaring mistakes. A stoneware gin flask showing the young Queen calls her Queen *Alexandrina* Victoria (this is perhaps permissible, the manufacturer may well have prepared the piece in expectation of William's death: and it was not until she signed 'Victoria' at her first Privy Council that it became clear that the little Princess Drina had turned into Her Majesty Queen Victoria). And all the known transferred pieces get her date of birth wrong, giving it as May the 25th 1819, whereas in fact she was born on May the 24th.

90. The back of a finely modelled gin-flask, made by Bournes Potteries. Note the inscription which perhaps indicates that it was made before the Accession when it was still uncertain how the potential Queen would describe herself.

91. This transfer appears on both mugs and jugs, often printed in blue. Although uncaptioned, it must be of the Accession/Coronation period.

Nor was her Coronation, on June the 29th 1838, much more prolifically recorded. Mugs, jugs and plates – particularly children's plates – were all made. But a Victorian Coronation mug is now one of the rarer late commemorative pieces available, and for both Proclamation and Coronation pieces only three known transfers were generally used.

The two more common of the three both show a bust of Victoria, with bun and ringlets, looking to sinister, wearing a low-cut dress with necklace and pendant. The differences in the transfers lie in the necklace. One transfer shows it coming straight around her neck and ending in a plain round pendant; the other shows a linked necklace bending around the neck and ending in a distinctly scalloped pendant. The former is the Swansea transfer, having been seen on

93. A matched pair of children's plates, made in Staffordshire rather than Wales. Note the way the necklace loops as it falls over Victoria's shoulders and compare this with the straight fall of the necklace on the Welsh mug shown in colour plate.

94. A very rare 'local' Coronation mug. These were usually given away at celebration dinners, often to the children of the estate workers. By courtesy of the Harris Museum and Art Gallery, Preston.

marked Swansea pieces; the latter, never having been seen on a marked piece, is assumed to be Staffordshire.

The third transfer shows Victoria, in three-quarter figure, sometimes with an arm outstretched and a rose in her hand. Again there is the low-cut dress but this time she has a triple string of pearls, and her hair is plaited in a bun high on her head with no ringlets. Usually this transfer when found on a mug or jug is accompanied on the reverse by a bust portrait of her mother, the Duchess of Kent, wearing the most splendid 'garden-party' hat.

There are also two prints which, although they do not give dates, must surely be regarded as Accession prints because of their inscriptions.

1. Seen on mugs and jugs, of varying sizes, a blue transfer of the young Queen, in waist-length portrait. She is looking slightly to dexter, and is wearing a veil, earrings and a several-stranded necklace, and a shawl draped over one shoulder. In the background is Windsor Castle and across

the top a scroll with the simple inscription "Victoria Regina".

2. Seen only once by the authors: on a plate of 21.25cm diameter, the usual Staffordshire portrait, but waist-length instead of only head-and-shoulders and with some background detail, plus an extremely bold black-and-white border formed by a cartouche of Royal Flowers with the addition of the Lion at one side, and the Crown at the top, and the inscription "Hail Victoria".

There are several transfers and mouldings of the young Victoria, which appear without any wording and therefore cannot be regarded as certain Coronation pieces. And there are also a number of gin flasks, one of which has on its reverse side the Duchess of Kent in her garden-party hat.

Lastly, there are a few very rare local Coronation mugs, obviously given to school children on the day. One of the most charming of these, marked 'Davenport', features a unique profile transfer of the Queen set in a circular panel around which is the inscription "Queen Victoria Crowned 28 June 1838". Beneath this, and spreading right around the mug, are the words "Success to the Town and Trade of Preston". This same view of Victoria, incidentally, appears on an equally rare moulded plate, with a moulded alphabet border, and the moulded caption "Queen Victoria".

Once safely crowned, Victoria's popularity seems to have grown steadily greater.

Then, in 1840, she set the seal on national enthusiasm. She fell in love. And married.

Albert and Victoria were wed in the Chapel Royal, St James's Palace, on February the 10th 1840. The Prince wore full military uniform. The Queen wore a wedding dress with deep ruffles of Honiton lace at the breast (a sure method of identification as to whether a piece is genuinely celebrating the marriage, or is just a general piece carrying portraits of the Queen and the Consort) and a veil held in place by a floral coronet (not a crown). This dress is today on show in the London Museum.

A great number of pieces were produced to celebrate this event, but the number of transfers is far more restricted.

The most widely known wedding transfer shows a half figure of Victoria, wearing wedding clothes, with Albert, on

95. Another 'local' mug, this one for "The Town and Trade of Preston". This is one of the very few marked Victoria Coronation pieces. It was made by Davenport. By courtesy of the Harris Museum and Art Gallery, Preston.

96. An unusual transfer of the pair at the time of the wedding: this has been recorded on both jugs and mugs but not on plates.

97. Another very rare wedding transfer: Albert, in particular, bears remarkably little resemblance to the original. Fortunately the jug is captioned "Victoria" and "Albert".

98. The most often seen Victoria and Albert wedding transfer. This plate is unusual because of its ABC border.

99. 100. A very rare pair of plates indeed. On the back they carry the mark "Manufactured for D Brandon, Kingston, Jamaica".

62

101. An interesting ABC plate of the young Queen. The moulding is very similar to that on 7″ high, white moulded jugs made by the Portmeirion pottery in the late 1960s; a nasty trap for the unwary collector.

102. Undated, but clearly of the Coronation period. The print is in brown and the floral border is very brilliantly enamelled in red, green and blue.

103. The only recorded moulded plaque of the young Victoria. It was possibly made in Scotland, and is, of course, expectionally rare.

104. These moulded jugs are usually decorated in a brilliant pale blue glaze. The design is quite clearly taken from the portrait of H.R.H. Princess Victoria, painted in 1833 by Sir G. Hayter.

105. Another royal puzzle. The Queen and the Prince are obviously at the theatre, probably the Opera House. But when did they go? And to see what? Despite an intensive study of contemporary magazines, nothing has yet provided even a clue to the mystery.

her right and half behind her, in military uniform. The inscription is "Queen Victoria and Prince Albert of Saxe Coburg. Married Feb^ry 10th 1840". The transfer appears on plates, mugs, and jugs in varying degrees of perfection, and not always with the full inscription.

Then there are two more primitive and more unusual transfers. One shows Victoria in bust profile, wearing tiara, and to her right Albert fully facing front. With it are the names Albert and Victoria, and the date of the wedding.

The second of these less sophisticated transfers, appearing chiefly on jugs, puts Albert on Victoria's left half facing her, and shows them as almost childlike. Indeed without the inscription on the front "Married Feb 10th 1840" they would be quite unrecognizable as Victoria and Albert. Victoria has

106. Typical early Victorian children's souvenirs. The bottom pair of plates was possibly made for dolls' houses.

64

longish hair brought down well over her ears, and Albert too has much lengthier hair and an altogether chubbier appearance than usual.

Moulded pieces commemorating the wedding, but without inscription, come in plenty. There are full figures of the couple appliqued to jugs in almost every size, glaze or colour. There are also some beautifully moulded bust portraits, named, on saltglazed stoneware flasks, ale jugs, tobacco jars, mugs, often with the royal coat of arms added.

Once safely married Victoria became a prolific bearer of children. Her first, Victoria Adelaide Mary Louise, the Princess Royal, was born on November the 21st 1840.

Strangely there appears to be nothing to commemorate either her birth or her christening at Buckingham Palace on February the 10th 1841 (exactly, as the sentimental will note, one year after the wedding). There is however a most delightful and rare mug showing the baby's pony carriage against a background of Windsor Castle, with, inside, the words "Princess Victoria Adelaide Mary Louisa".

There is also a green transferred bowl showing a proud Victoria and Albert with, in the background, a nurse and a crib – presumably holding their first child. The bowl is marked "Royal Family" in a Royal-Flower-and-ribbon cartouche. The only example of this the authors have seen is in the Liverpool Museum and was dredged up from the Irish Sea in 1938.

A year later Albert Edward Prince of Wales was born, on November the 9th 1841. Both his birth and his christening were definitely commemorated. For his birth there was published a series of children's plates with, on the rim, the moulded inscription "Albert Edward, Prince of Wales, Born November the 9th 1841". The central transfers on these plates seem, curiously enough, to have no bearing whatever on the occasion, and range from childhood scenes to the Crucifixion.

His christening, which took place at Windsor on January the 10th 1842, is commemorated by a transfer of the actual happening, showing the family and clergy grouped around the font with the captions "Britain's Heir", and "Royal Christening of the Prince of Wales".

107. This was probably made as a pair to a plate of Victoria, at the time of the wedding.

108. A rare miniature plate of Albert, usually printed in brown.

65

109. The caption inside this very rare brown-printed mug reads: "Princess Victoria Adelaide Mary Louisa". It was, presumably, made at the time of the birth/christening of the Princess Royal (see plate 111).

Then followed:
Alice – 25th April 1843
Alfred (Duke of Edinburgh) – 6th August 1844
Helen – 25th May 1846
Louise – 18th March 1848
Arthur (Duke of Connaught) – 1st May 1850
Leopold (Duke of Albany) – 7th April 1853
Beatrice – 14th April 1857

None of these births was, as far as is known, specifically commemorated. But into this period comes a real puzzle transfer. This shows a bishop christening a child while the parents kneel before him on a curious sausage-shaped cushion and is encaptioned "The Bishop of Heliopolis". The same transfer has been seen with the inscription "Royal Christening". But who was the Bishop of Heliopolis? And what Royal Christening was it? All research done both by the authors and the staff of the Lambeth Palace library has not been able to come up with the answer.

There were also published, at this period, a wide selection

110. An extremely rare bowl, now in the Liverpool Museum. It was dredged up from the Irish Channel. By courtesy of the City of Liverpool Museum.

111. A remarkable mug produced for the christening of the Prince of Wales: the same transfer has been recorded on a plate.

of transfers featuring the Queen alone or the Queen with the Prince which are not particularized to any date or event.

The most usual, generally seen on octagonal daisy plates, shows a transfer of the Queen in crown and State robes walking in a garden (Kensington Gardens?). The caption reads, simply: "Queen Victoria".

Less common are:

1. The young Queen sitting on a sofa and rather coyly resting her chin on her right hand (this is from a miniature by R. Thorburn, A.R.A., in the Royal Collection). This print has no caption, but the piece is marked 'V R J J'.

2. A young, rather delicate Victoria half turned away, looking back over her shoulder.

3. A stark, half length figure of Victoria with the initials 'VR' and no other embellishments (seen only on a plain undecorated daisy plate).

4. A very fine print of Victoria surrounded by a detailed bouquet cartouche of Royal Flowers, plus the caption "Queen Victoria".

112. A marked Welsh piece: the Royal pair visited Place House in 1846 – but not, curiously, on September the 6th as the plate would have one believe.

67

113. A most unusual transfer of the Princess Royal and her husband. Compare this with the plate of the Prince and Princess of Hesse (plate 125).

5. Victoria on horseback, her horse lively and prancing and she with a veil flowing out behind her. The inscription reads: "Victoria I Queen of Great Britain and Ireland". Similar pieces, often miniature, are simply captioned "Victoria". There is also a fine transfer of Victoria and Albert riding together. Victoria is generally shown riding a grey, Albert a black horse.

6. An interesting Victoria and Albert transfer which surely must commemorate some specific event but which, as it gives no clues, simply cannot be pinned down. It shows Albert in dress uniform and Victoria in court dress and tiara against a background of what would appear to be a theatre box.

There are also two transfers of Albert alone:

1. Appearing on a 15.00cm diameter plate, with a moulded flower border, and a central purple transfer of the Prince. shows a head and shoulders portrait of him, looking to dexter, in uniform with the simple caption "Prince Albert" above his head. The piece is marked 'Dillwyn Swansea'.

2. A tiny plate, diameter 8.00cm, with the central black transfer spreading over the plate rim. It shows a waist-length portrait of the Prince looking to sinister, again in uniform and decorations. The portrait is resting on a bold swag of Royal Flowers.

Victoria appears to have enjoyed travel and in the summer of 1846 she and her family made, in the royal yacht, an extensive tour of the Duchy of Cornwall and the Channel Islands. On September the 8th, to quote *The Times* of September the 11th, 'Her Majesty returned through Lostwithiel, where a loyal address was presented by the inhabitants, and returned to Fowey at half past 2 o'clock, stopping to examine the beautiful residence of Mr. Trefoy' (this should, correctly, be spelt Treffry).

To commemorate this visit, though why it, of all the myriad royal excursions, was thought to be worth commemorating is a total mystery, the Swansea factory produced both a mug and a plate; the latter with a moulded floral edge. Both are marked 'Dillwyn Swansea' and both carry a black transfer is correctly encaptioned "Royal visit to Place House, Fowey, September 6 1846", and show the royal carriage driving up to the house.

68

The next specific event to be ceramically commemorated was the marriage of the Princess Royal.

The Princess first became engaged to the Crown Prince of Prussia in the summer of 1855, when she was only fifteen. The marriage took place two and a half years later, on Monday, January the 25th 1858, in the old chapel of St James's Palace. The Prince wore full military uniform, the Princess a flower-embroidered dress with a coronet of flowers in her hair. The honeymoon was spent at Windsor and the royal couple then took up residence in Prussia.

The most common transfer of this marriage – indeed it is probably one of the most common commemorative pieces short of the Jubilee to be found – shows the couple standing side by side encaptioned "The Prince and Princess of Prussia". It appears on mugs, jugs, and indeed entire tea services, usually poorly done, and often coupled with a picture of the Prussian royal palace. More unusual and much more detailed

114. A typical, lustre-decorated, porcelainous tea service commemorating the marriage of the Princess Royal to the Crown Prince of Prussia. The building is the German Royal Palace.

115. The front of a rare jug commemorating the visit, in 1860, of the Prince of Wales to Canada; this was his first engagement.

is a transfer showing half-length portraits of the couple. It is not captioned, and would appear to be made by a factory which then produced similar transfers for her brothers' and sisters' weddings later in the century.

Two years after his sister married, in the autumn of 1860, the Prince of Wales carried out his first important royal duty – an official tour of Canada and an unofficial visit to the U.S.A.

This trip was commemorated by a rather rare moulded dryware jug. This has a portrait of Victoria on one side, of Albert on the other, and of the young Prince of Wales on the front. The lip is fashioned around the plume of feathers and the date, 1860.

There is also a transfer of a statue of the young Prince in military uniform on horseback, seen on a range of very fine punch bowls, which may well have been produced at this time: H.R.H. was first gazetted to military rank on his eighteenth birthday in the previous winter.

The following year Prince Alfred, Victoria's second son, came home from his foreign cruise. Alfred had entered the Navy

116. A very fine punch bowl, possibly made in 1859, when the Prince came of age and was first gazetted to military rank, or in 1860 to celebrate the Royal tour of Canada.

70

REGINA

1819
1837
1838

A Victorian coronation mug carrying the Swansea transfer

in August 1858, and was appointed to H.M.S. *Euryalus*, a fifty-gun, screw-propelled frigate in which he cruised first to the Mediterranean, then to South Africa, and so on to the West Indies, returning to England in August 1861. To celebrated Alfred's return from foreign climes some enterprising potter produced a charming 22.5cm plate, purple printed with a rim decoration of ropes and anchors and, in the body of the plate, the figure of the young prince on the quayside, flanked by tropical trees, with *Euryalus* in the background. Above in a ribbon cartouche is "Welcome" and below, in a similar cartouche the word "Alfred" surmounted by "Prince" and with the date – 1861 – below all. The plate is extremely rare, and this transfer is not known to appear on any other item.

The next royal event to be commemorated was the death of Albert.

At first blush one might think that such a totally shattering occurrence would have resulted in a positive tidal-wave of commemorative pieces.

But a moment's reflection and a few hours' reading of the contemporary newspapers will show otherwise. For here was an event so sudden, so sad and so totally solemn that it was to the Victorian potter beyond the merely human excitements that commemorative ware should or could portray.

Albert died, at Windsor, soon after 11 p.m. on Saturday, December the 14th 1861 of typhoid (which, considering that a contemporary report on the drains of Windsor Castle says 'the noxious effluvia which escapes from the old drains and the numerous cesspools still remaining, is frequently so exceedingly offensive as to render many parts of the Castle almost uninhabitable', is not altogether as surprising a cause of death as it would at first seem).

But Victoria never fully accepted the doctors' verdict: she believed that the news of the Prince of Wales' excesses with the young actress Nellie Clifden had so shattered his father actually to cause his death. But, unbalanced as this idea was, it must be borne in mind that 1861 was a bad year for Victoria: not only did she lose Albert, but in March the Duchess of Kent had died at Frogmore.

Pieces commemorating Albert's death are rare, and on the

117. One of the rarest of all souvenirs of Victoria's children. The transfer has been recorded solely on this particular plate, one example only of which is known to exist.

118. Variously sized dry-ware jugs like this were made to mark the death of Albert. Many of them have a plated lid (see the two pin holes in the neck).

119. These tazzas were produced, printed in either orange or green, for the Art Union of London by Copeland. Although they were not made until 1863, they are certainly the most impressive and comprehensive pieces produced to lament the Death of Albert. By courtesy of the Victoria and Albert Museum.

(*Crown Copyright*)

whole dwell considerably on his achievements rather than on the death itself. There is a very fine jug, green-transferred, which shows a portrait of Albert with the 1851 Exhibition, his brain-child, in the background and on the reverse the same portrait with the 1862 Exhibition in the background. (There were, of course, a very considerable number of different transfers published to commemorate the Great Exhibition, at the time of its opening; and indeed for the later 1862 Exhibition).

There is a large tazza, 37.5cm in diameter, with either a green-and-cream or orange-and-cream background and brown-and-black transferring. In three panels this shows three fields of Albert's achievements. The captions are as follows:

Arts: Albert Promoter of the Arts
Science: President of Societies for Science
Literature: Chancellor of an University
Between these, winged figures hold three symbols of his

72

achievements – "Osborne – The Island Palace Home 1860", "The Palace of Legislature 1855" and "The Palace of Industry of All Nations 1851". Around the whole is an excerpt from his first speech, on May the 18th 1848.

This piece was commissioned from Copeland by the Art Union of London and it is so marked. The Art Union was a society to which a large number of people subscribed; with the money so provided the Union commissioned each year a variety of pieces, a few of which were very expensive, and rather more of which were quite cheap. The subscribers then entered a ballot. Most, presumably, got nothing. Some lucky ones got the expensive pieces, others the cheaper. These platters, clearly, fell into the latter class.

Last, there is a range of moulded jugs with on the one side a profile portrait of the Prince, encaptioned "Prince Consort" and on the other his full coat of arms, encaptioned "Born Augt 26 1819, Died Decr 14 1861" The jugs are further embellished with the Prince's various orders and decorations.

With the death of Albert, Victoria's zest for royal (and so commemoratively possible) events ceased altogether. And, right up to the time of her first Jubilee in 1887, there was virtually no Victoria royal ware published.

However, 1863 saw the marriage of the Prince of Wales to Princess Alexandra, eldest daughter of Prince Christian of Schleswig-Holstein-Sonderburg-Glücksburg. The Prince and Princess were married on March the 10th in St George's Chapel, Windsor. The Prince wore military uniform and the cloak of the order of the Garter, the Princess a many-flounced dress and tiara and veil. Curiously, though, almost all wedding ware shows the couple not in bridal dress: he is more usually dressed in civilian clothes and she in morning gown. Possibly the pieces were put out before the marriage to cash-in on the month's sales between the announcement of the engagement and the actual wedding.

The most usual transfer shows half-figure pictures of the Prince and Princess arm in arm, beneath the plume of feathers and the inscription "The Prince and Princess of Wales". This is found chiefly on plates, but also on some fine tankards. On other mugs and jugs the same portraits appear separated – the Prince on one side, the Princess on the reverse,

120. A detail from a very rare jug published at the time of Albert's death and showing him as the creator of the 1851 exhibition and the inspiration of the one held in 1862.

121. An extremely unusual mourning plate: the number of pieces produced for the death of Albert was surprisingly small.

122. Plates to celebrate the wedding of the Prince of Wales are, comparatively, quite easy to find. Mugs and jugs usually carry a pair of transfers, with the Prince on one side and Alexandra on the other.

123. A not uncommon moulded jug made to celebrate the wedding of Edward and Alexandra: it carries the diamond mark for the appropriate timing.

and in this case the Prince's portrait is in a cartouche of Royal Flowers, the Princess's in a cartouche of snowdrops.

Other portraits include two which appear separately on a cup and saucer – with the inscriptions "Princess of Wales; England's Future Queen" and "Prince of Wales, England's Future King".

The Prince of Wales is also commemorated on one of the late Victorian octagonal plates, as is his son the Duke of Clarence and Avondale.

Then, in 1887, came the first of the two jubilees. Jubilee day itself was on June the 21st, when Victoria drove in State procession to Westminster Abbey to attend a thanksgiving service, in a pageant which had not been equalled since her Coronation. It would be quite impossible to list the pieces produced to celebrate this event, the permutations would run to quite unmanageable length, even though they were few compared with the incredible number made ten years later.

Ten years later came the Diamond Jubilee. Queen Victoria had broken all records.

Sixty glorious years were celebrated with a fervour and extravagance fitting to the age. The actual Jubilee day itself was on June the 22nd, and ample warning was given of the event. On March the 18th the Queen 'proclaimed':

Victoria, R – We, considering that it is desirable that Tuesday, the twenty-second day of June next, should be observed as a Bank Holiday throughout the United Kingdom, do hereby, by and with the advice of Our Privy Council, and in pursuance of the Bank Holidays Act, 1831, appoint Tuesday, the twenty-second day of June next, as a special day to be observed as a Bank Holiday throughout the United Kingdom, and every part thereof, and we do by this Our Royal Proclamation command the said day to be so observed, and all Our loving subjects to order themselves accordingly.

And so they did. And commemorated it with such a mass of plates and mugs, and jugs and cups, and even toastracks, that no full list can ever be compiled.

But of all the Jubilee ware, both Golden and Diamond, there are perhaps four which one might isolate as deserving special mention. First, various local plates to commemorate

124. A fairly unusual wedding souvenir: the slogan "England's future King" also appears on a transfer showing three of the Royal children, probably produced in 1851. By courtesy of the Harris Museum and Art Gallery Preston.

125. A rare plate, made presumably to celebrate the wedding, in 1862, of Princess Alice to the then Prince of Hesse. The potter has, however, called the Prince "Frederick Guillaume", whereas his name was in fact Louis – perhaps a confusion with Frederick William of Prussia, who married the Princess Royal (see plates 113/114).

126. Part of a tea service made to celebrate the wedding of Leopold Duke of
Albany, Victoria's youngest son, to
Princess Helena. This is a very rare item
indeed.

the celebration of the event by such entertainments as ox-
roasting. A typical example is the one from Whittle-le-Woods,
showing in the centre a large ox's head and on the rim the
inscription "An Ox was Publically Roasted Whole on the
Village Green In Commemoration of Her Most Gracious
Majesty's Jubilee June 21st 1887".

Secondly, a plate particularly interesting because it bears
the profile portrait of Albert – dead since 1861. The portrait
is in a circlet surrounded by a wreath with the inscription
above in ribbon cartouche "1837 Jubilee Year 1887", and
below "The Prince Consort". This is the only Jubilee piece
the authors have seen with Albert's portrait.

The third is of interest because it is one of the more finely
potted pieces, with gilt-edge decoration and polychrome
moulded border. In the centre top is a moulded portrait of
Victoria with the inscription "V R Accession 1837 Diamond
Jubilee 1897". On the base it is marked "Copeland/Spode"

76

127. Another Royal wedding souvenir; this time the marriage of Alfred (the homecomer in plate 117) Duke of Edinburgh to Maria of Russia.

128. This very rare mug commemorates, curiously starkly, the wedding of the youngest of all Victoria's children. She married Prince Prince Henry of Battenberg and, incidentally, died as recently as 1944.

129. This jug carries on the one side the Marquis of Lorne (later Duke of Argyll) and on the other Princess Louise. They married on March the 21st 1871.

130. One of the series of octagonal plates that commemorated so many late Victorian notables. They are usually black printed, and sometimes also decorated with colour.

131. The Prince of Wales' elder son, the backward Albert Victor. This particular souvenir commemorates the opening of the Victoria Hospital Burnley in 1886.

132. Pieces to commemorate the silver wedding of the Prince of Wales, 1888, are surprisingly rare; perhaps because the potters were exhausted by the first of the jubilees.

133. Two very interesting slip-decorated 'art nouveaux' pieces. The loving-cup commemorates the birth of Edward VIII. The spill vase commemorates something that the Duke and Duchess of York did in July 1899. But as they were both in Scotland apparently doing nothing, what it was the authors do not know.

134. A pair for the Golden Jubilee. The plate on the left is a perpetual and sad trap for unwary collectors who erroneously believe they have found an Accession souvenir.

135. A very rare Golden Jubilee transfer, unprecedented in that it features Albert, whom no potter had dared to revive since his death.

136. Ox-roasting is quite a common thing to find on commemorative ware: Sundry towns honoured the jubilees this way. By courtesy of the Harris Museum and Art Gallery, Preston.

137. A particularly fine example of a Diamond Jubilee souvenir. On to one plate is packed almost every event and person and notable place of the reign.

138. Perhaps the best quality Diamond Jubilee plate made: the moulding on the head and the ribbon cartouche is quite superb.

139. Another plate packed with ideas for the Diamond Jubilee: this one is most concerned with sport, and carries some delightfully absurd little sketches.

140. A slight cheat, in that it was made in 1901: pieces commemorating Victoria's death are surprisingly scarce, but perhaps the disaster of the Boer War and the unprecedented output of 1897 combined to make the potters feel the public were not in a liberal mood for Royal souvenirs.

(impressed) and "Daniel, Wigmore St., London" (printed).

Finally there is one which causes heartbreak to many an unsuspecting collector. This plate shows the young Queen and carries the date 1837. It is, however, not a proclamation plate. A close scrutiny of the pottery and style will show it to be the pair to a plate that carries a portrait of the old Queen, and shows the Jubilee date.

And so the century and the old Queen died, leaving the collector to turn his attention to what is beyond the scope of this book, the great and most interesting assortment of pieces published for Edward's Coronation.

3
Naval and Military People and Events

In 1780 Britain was at war with her American colonists and with their allies the Spanish, the French and the Dutch.

And at sea things, commemoratively speaking, happened almost immediately. As early as January the 16th 1780 Admiral Rodney met and defeated the Spanish Fleet off Cape St Vincent.

Admittedly, there is nothing known to have been specifically produced to celebrate this battle. But there are a number of general 'Rodney' pieces which must have been published at or about this time. One, for instance, incorporates a map of Spain – which is surely a fair hint. Another, at Greenwich, has a charmingly naive portrait of the Admiral and is encaptioned "Success to Brave Rodney".

On creamware bowls and jugs a black print shows the Admiral in naval uniform looking to sinister, with a ribbon cartouche in which is written "Sir Geo [or G] Bridges Rodney Bt Rear Admiral of England". This is usually surrounded by a design of flags and cannons and laurel leaves. There is, on occasion, the ancillary slogan "Success to the British Fleet". A creamware ship bowl (in the Liverpool museum) which carries one of these prints is dated 1782 and was, perhaps, issued just after the news of his victory at the Battle of the Saintes on April the 12th reached England. For this battle there were also made certain rather rough pottery bowls and mugs with applique figures of Rodney, of Hood (who was his second in command) and the *Ville de Paris*, the French flagship. A bowl in the Willett Collection also has the applied figure of General Sir George Elliot, the hero of Gibraltar.

Other Rodney pieces (which almost certainly fall before the 1780 deadline) are blue painted delft plates, usually 13.5cm in

141. A rare delft plate, published for Admiral Rodney. It may have been produced after either the battle of St Vincent or the battle of the Saintes, but it is more likely to be an electioneering plate, probably made for the Northampton election, when Rodney contested the seat in 1768.

142. A particularly beautiful creamware mug decorated in marble glaze. The green appliqué decoration reads "Success to Admiral Rodney and his fleet". The mug is almost certainly commemorative of the Saintes.

diameter, crudely painted with a barely recognizable head-and-shoulders portrait of the Admiral and inscribed "Admiral Rodney for Ever" and which may well be electioneering plates.

One last individual piece which must be mentioned is a superb 15.00cm high creamware tankard, decorated with agate glazes, with a green ribbed 'rim' to top and base and with, in the front, a similarly green-glazed appliqué portrait of Rodney looking to sinister, set inside a medallion cartouche, with, on flowing ribbons above, the moulded inscription "Success to Admiral Rodney and his fleet".

The next definitive piece is not such a happy one. By 1781 things in America were going very badly for the British. The chief disaster was that on October the 4th Lord Cornwallis, who had fallen back on Virginia and entrenched himself in the lines of Yorktown, was forced to surrender.

A black transfer of this scene, showing Cornwallis surrendering his sword to Washington, is to be seen on a variety of creamware pieces. However, rather like the Duke of York and Valenciennes, this transfer can be a problem one: although undoubtedly it was originally produced as a genuine commemorative publication, because of its popularity in the United States it continued to be used as general decoration well into the nineteenth century. Once again, collectors must judge the authenticity of the piece more from the style and type of pottery and from the ancillary decoration, if any, than from the Cornwallis print.

Next, and arising directly from the War of Independence and the need to send more and more troops to the Americas, there came, in the early '80s, the formation of the Irish Volunteers.

Numerous creamware jugs were published to celebrate the Volunteers, most of them mentioning individual corps and obviously produced in a nicely balanced mixture both to commemorate and publicize. A typical transfer would read something like "Success to the Independent Killarney Volunteers" and might well have the slogan surrounded by a cartouche of military symbols. Some of these jugs may have been made in Ireland – there were creamware potteries believed to have been operating in both Dublin and Belfast

around this period. But almost certainly the majority will have been manufactured in Liverpool or in the potteries and perhaps printed in Liverpool, and then shipped over.

By the end of 1782 the war was over and peace was signed with the newly emergent America and with France, Spain and Holland. But before the cessation of war, and the consequent cessation of naval and/or military pieces, one more military epic must be mentioned. Right from the start of the war – to be precise from August 1779 – to the end, Gibraltar withstood a constant siege. Its Governor was a bigoted vegetarian eccentric called General Sir George Augustus Elliot (sometimes spelt Eliot). He repulsed attack after attack after attack. And he steadfastly withstood terrible shortages of supplies which were convoyed to him at only very irregular intervals.

143. A very fine example of early printing on creamware. Like so many early commemorative pieces it is impossible to be precise about date and intention. But as this particular bowl is dated 1782 it was most likely made for the Battle of the Saintes. The transfer, however, may originally have been published in 1771, when Rodney was appointed Rear Admiral of Great Britain. By courtesy of the City of Liverpool Museums.

144. Possibly the rarest Rodney item yet recorded. With the date 1781 it must have been made to celebrate Rodney's capture of St Eustatius in January of that year, for during the remainder of 1781 he did nothing which would conceivably have been commemorated.

145. A very rare print of General O'Hara just before being taken prisoner by the French: on the obverse of the jug is a print of the Duke of York at Valenciennes, which positions the jug as a product of later 1793 or early 1794. (See plate 33.)

Finally on Friday, September the 13th 1782, the combined French and Spanish forces launched their Grand Attack; fortified by their new 'secret weapon', a series of supposedly unsinkable and indestructible floating gun batteries.

The attack was a total failure. The gun batteries all burnt, and the affray ended, as Elliot reported, in " . . . a compleat victory".

There is one quite superb bowl known to have been produced to celebrate Elliot's epic feats, and indeed perhaps, produced for either Elliot himself or some other co-habitant of the siege.

The bowl is of comparatively rough pot, but beautifully painted, rather in the David Rhodes manner, in polychrome palette, showing on the one side a soldier (Elliot?) standing by a smoking cannon, and on the other one of his famous gun-boats, manned by four oarsmen and with a gunner actually firing the bow gun. Inside is the simply painted slogan "Elliot for ever". The bowl is 24.35cm diameter and 11.25cm high.

With the end of the war, Britain entered a period of calm: a calm that was, in terms of ceramic commemoration, to last up to the French Revolution and the war with France.

The Revolution was at first regarded with moderate favour, particularly by the more radical Whigs. But by November 1792 the President of the French Convention was declaiming "all Governments are our enemies, all people are our allies", and the French Government had instructed its generals to attack Holland. This England could not tolerate: a French fleet at Antwerp was anathema to the British insistence on control of the seas. Diplomatic communications hardened, and in February 1793 France issued her Declaration of War.

There is nothing known actually to commemorate the outbreak of war. But there are a number of pieces which were undoubtedly made about this time and which carry all the appropriate sentiments of loyalty to 'CROWN and CONSTITUTION'.

Notable amongst these are:

(a) A blue-and-white printed bowl, on the inside of which

is a finely printed transfer of George III looking to dexter, surrounded by an involved design of martial elements; flags, guns, swords etc., and encaptioned in bold lettering above and below "May our King live long and British valour strong".

(b) A blue transferred miniature spirit flask, with a very similar portrait of George III to (a), flanked by the bold initials "G.R.", surrounded by a decorative leaf and chain cartouche, below which, and above a bold spray of laurel wreath, is the slogan "Let your voices Ring, Long Live George our King". On the obverse of the flask an unnamed man dispenses good cheer from a variety of bottles and flasks, the print encaptioned "I'll fill your Bowls, you loyal souls". The flask, which is 10.00cm high, is almost certainly of Liverpool pot and print.

(c) A creamware mug, 7.5cm high by 6.85cm diameter, black printed, showing, running round the entirety of the piece a 'puzzle picture', encaptioned above "A new puzzle of portraits" and below "Striking likenesses of the King and Queen of England and the late King and Queen of France". This is usually claimed to be made in Swansea.

There are also a number of other transfers showing portraits of King George III and Queen Charlotte and encaptioned "King and Constitution". These were almost certainly originally produced at this time. On the other hand pieces carrying them may well not have been made until the further outbreak of war after the collapse of the Peace of Amiens, or even, without the anti-Jacobim caption, not until 1809 and the Grand National Jubilee.

Once the war had got going, Britain's immediate activities were entirely military rather than naval, and since the force was under the command of H.R.H. the Duke of York, the various pieces published to commemorate this campaign have already been dealt with in the chapter on 'Royals'.

But in 1794 England exulted over her first proof that Britain did indeed rule the waves.

On May the 28th 1794 the Home Fleet, commanded by Lord Howe from H.M.S. *Queen Charlotte*, sighted 'a large strange fleet to windward'. This was a mixed convoy of grain ships from America with an escort commanded by Rear-

146. This transfer of the Glorious 1st of June has been recorded both on this superb creamware plate and on a creamware jug. In both cases it is black-printed.

A Representation of the Glorious Defeat of the French Fleet off Brest by Earl Howe June the 1st 1794.

Admiral Villaret Joyeuse. All that day the two fleets jockeyed for position, until at about half past nine, beset by failing light and rising wind, the action was broken off.

Contact, however, was kept and the next day sporadic individual actions took place.

But Howe's luck was out. All the next day, and the next, fog hid the enemy fleet.

However, June the 1st, 'The Glorious First of June', was clear. The action began at 8.0 a.m. and it lasted until about 2.0 in the afternoon. Howe's fleet broke the French battle line in no less than six places and destroyed seven of Villaret Joyeuse's fleet.

To commemorate the battle a number of black-printed creamware pieces was produced.

The commonest transfer is a scene of the battle (differing however in detail on each piece the authors have seen) and

The inside of the bowl reads 'Elliot for Ever'

on at least one jug and one plate encaptioned "A representation of the Glorious defeat of the French Fleet of [f] Brest by Earl Howe, June the 1st 1794". The final 'f' is missing on both pieces.

Another transfer, which occurs on an exceptionally fine Leeds jug as the obverse to a battle transfer, shows a medallion portrait of Howe looking to dexter set upon the top of an elaborate cartouche of Neptune and other sea-dwellers, within which is the inscription "Long Live Earl Howe Commander in Chief of the victorious British Fleet in the ever memorable Engagement on the Glorious first of June 1794". This slogan is also on the obverse of a jug which carries a fine portrait of the admiral, telescope in hand, apparently looking over a ship's rail.

Finally, there is a very fine and stern portrait of Howe, the admiral dressed in uniform and cocked hat, his body facing to sinister, but his head twisted to look straight out of the transfer. The portrait is encaptioned "Right Honble Earl Howe, Commander of His Majesty's Fleet in the channel". (This mug may not, in fact, commemorate the battle, but may have been published on Howe's appointment to the Home Fleet in 1793.)

But despite this early success at sea, the war was going badly for Britain, and at the start of 1797 she was faced with a formidable coalition of the French, Dutch and Spanish fleets.

However, that year saw two further overwhelming British victories, the battles of St Vincent and of Camperdown.

The first took place on February the 14th.

On the 13th Commodore Nelson, who had been escorting a convoy to Gibraltar, sighted, off the Straits, the Spanish fleet under Admiral Don Joseph de Cordova. Nelson hurriedly sailed on to meet the English fleet under Jervis; and before sunset Admiral Jervis made the signal to prepare for action.

At daybreak the Spanish fleet was in sight. Cordova had been told by a passing American that the English fleet consisted of only nine vessels: he therefore determined to engage them; but, believing them to be only a small force, allowed his fleet to become widely dispersed.

Jervis, in the *Victory*, noticing this, crowded on sail and cut the Spanish battle line into two unequal portions, the main

147. A very rare print of Lord Howe: it may, of course, have been made to celebrate the battle of the Glorious 1st of June. Alternatively, it could note his appointment as C-in-C Channel in 1793.

148. A very fine portrait print of Sir John Jervis, hero of the battle of St Vincent. It was at this battle that Nelson first came to the notice of the British press and public.

body and a divorced nine; this nine never entering the battle until the very close of the action. And, then, once he had split the Spaniards, Jervis made the signal to tack in succession so as to engage the main Spanish fleet.

Nelson, however, who was in the very rear of the British line, seeing that the Spanish fleet was bearing up before the wind, and so had a very good chance either of escaping or of reassembling with the other nine ships, ignored the signal and immediately engaged the Spanish fleet, supported only by H.M.S. *Culloden*, H.M.S. *Blenheim*, and H.M.S. *Excellent*. And it was these four that halted the evasion of the Spanish fleet and allowed Jervis to inflict a major defeat on the Spaniards.

For their parts in the battle, Nelson was awarded the Order of the Bath, and, coincidentally, promoted to rear-admiral; Sir John Jervis was elevated to the peerage as Earl St Vincent, a title chosen for him personally by the King, and which he signed for the first time on July the 16th.

There are two known transfers celebrating the actual battle and one celebrating the man.

This latter is a very finely executed head-and-shoulders portrait showing Earl St Vincent looking very slightly to sinister. The Admiral is bareheaded and wearing naval uniform. The portrait is enclosed in a simple 'picture-frame' oval cartouche, and encaptioned "Earl St Vincent". The authors have seen this transfer only twice: once on an 11.25cm high creamware mug, printed in iron-red, secondly on a rather coarsely potted jug, probably of Staffordshire origin, printed in purple.

The known 'Battle' transfers consist of:

A fine bust portrait of the Admiral, surrounded by triumphal laurels, encaptioned within a ribbon cartouche "Sir John Jervis", and with the inscription "By their Matchless Hero led / British Tars dealt home the blow / shrunk the hopes of Spain a-head / Laid her haughty streamers low".

A bust portrait of the Admiral looking to sinister, contained within a simple oval cartouche, encaptioned "Sir John Jervis, K.B. Admiral of the Blue", the whole contained within a most elaborate cartouche of the symbols of war, listing all St Vincent's achievements, with, set below the

88

EARL ST VINCENT.

149. The only known transfer of St Vincent that has no allusion to the battle. It appears in only two recorded forms, once red- and once purple-printed, in both cases on mugs.

portrait, "You have heard of a Howard, a Hawkins, a Drake, of a Raleigh, Hawke, Russel, Howe, Rodney & Blake / But here is a man off St Vincent you'll find him / Who leaves these brave tars at a distance behind him".

The next great British victory happened at Camperdown.

In October Admiral Duncan had the Dutch bottled up in the Texel. But in the second week very rough seas and very high winds caused him to lose control of the blockade and the Dutch, seizing their chance, put to sea.

Duncan immediately gave chase, and on October the 11th sighted the Dutch fleet off Camperdown. Intrepidly Duncan sailed his fleet in between the Dutch and the lee shore, and over the coastal shallows: cut off from the haven of the Texel the Dutch were forced to fight. In the ensuing battle over two thirds of the Dutch fleet was destroyed, and the Dutch

150. A superb painted and gilded creamware jug featuring Duncan, the architect
of Camperdown. Another jug painted
and cold-water gilded in a remarkably
similar style carries a portrait of George
III, and is dated 1788. By courtesy of the
City of Liverpool Museums.

flagship and the Dutch admiral were both captured.

Duncan and Camperdown excited slightly more variety of ware from the potters than had the two previous great naval victories.

Certainly the most striking piece the authors have yet seen is a large creamware jug, 26.25cm high by 10.6cm diameter, painted in a very vivid polychrome palette, and gilded, with on the one side a superb full-length portrait of the admiral in full uniform, complete with cocked hat and ribbon and star, and on the reverse a proud sailor, flag held in right hand, standing atop an allegorical design of the symbols of victory. The jug is now in the Liverpool Museum.

Another painted piece is a pearlware jug 13.75cm high by 5.6cm diameter, decorated on the one side with a ship in sail, on the other by a purely floral decoration, but with, on the front, inside an open cartouche of laurels, the inscription "Admiral Duncan for ever".

A third painted piece is a particularly finely painted portrait of the admiral looking to dexter, bareheaded but bewigged, painted to an oval shape, around which are arranged the words "Admiral Lord Duncan". This appears on a cream-ware mug 8.00cm high by 6.25cm diameter, with the ribbed top in green, pink and red which makes it virtually certain that this is a product of the Herculaneum factory.

The most elaborately transferred piece shows on the one side a portrait medallion of the admiral, topped by a ribbon cartouche inscribed "Lord Viscount Duncan" which, in its turn, is surmounted by a viscount's coronet, the ends of the cartouche being held by two mermen rising from a sea on which a battle is taking place; and on the obverse a spirited rendering of the battle showing a great number of ships engaged, the scene being capped by a laurel wreath and the words "The Glorious 11th of October 1797". The transfers appear on a creamware tankard 15.00cm high by 10.00cm diameter, printed in black. Another very fine print shows Duncan's *Venerable* towing the *Vryheid* and carries the splendid rhyme "Vain are the Boasts of Belgick's sons / When faced by British ships and guns / Tho' de Winter does in Autumn come / Brave Duncan brings his harvest home."

Last of the known Duncan pieces is a small creamware

mug, brown-printed and with the most beautiful and exact overprint polychrome enamelling. The piece is 11.85cm high, and shows the admiral in full uniform, set against a background of ships at war, the whole surrounded by a cartouche of cannons and anchors. Above, is the inscription "Admiral Lord Viscount Duncan", and below, "who defeated the Dutch fleet Oct 11 1797 God save the King – Huzza". The print is signed Aynsley of Lane End.

Next in this chronological order of British victories comes the first direct success of Nelson: the Battle of the Nile.

In 1797 Lord St Vincent, who was back blockading Cadiz, was instructed by the Admiralty to send a fleet into the Mediterranean. He dutifully ordered away Rear-Admiral Sir Horatio Nelson.

Meanwhile Napoleon, who had built up a considerable fleet at Toulon, dispatched it toward Egypt, via Malta, which it stopped off to capture on the way.

Nelson, hearing that the French fleet was at sea, set off in pursuit; overshot them; sailed back and, finding barren seas, sailed back again towards Egypt.

And, at long last, on August the 1st 1798 got from one of his leading ships, the *Zealous*, the welcome signal 'sixteen sail in Aboukir Bay'.

As Captain Sir Edward Berry reported: 'The position of the enemy presented the most formidable obstacles; but the Admiral [Nelson] viewed these with the eye of a seaman determined on attack, and it instantly struck his eager and penetrating mind, that where there was room for an enemy's ship to swing there was room for one of ours to anchor'.

So Nelson concentrating on the French van, sailed a vital few of his fleet *inside* the French and over the shallows.

'The action commenced at sun-set which was at thirty-one minutes past six p.m.', writes Berry. It continued all evening. At ten o'clock the French flagship blew up 'with a most tremendous explosion', and by 3.0 a.m. the fight was over.

All but two of the French fleet of the line were destroyed or struck and the French admiral was killed. A grateful country duly awarded Nelson a pension of £2,000 and created him Baron Nelson of the Nile and of Burnham Thorpe.

Since it was the first of Nelson's victories the Battle of the

151/152. Two sides of a fine creamware tankard, published to celebrate Camperdown in 1797. The one side carries a good likeness of Viscount Duncan, the other this most spirited version of the battle in progress (compare with plate 146, and the Glorious 1st of June).

153. A classic case of painting being virtually unrecognizable, presumably because the decorator had never seen the subject and was working off a poor reference. Fortunately the piece is en-captioned "Admiral Lord Duncan". By courtesy of City of Manchester Art Galleries, the Thomas Greg Collection.

154. A rare transfer of Nelson and the battle plan for the Nile.

Nile was somewhat sparsely commemorated.

Probably the most dramatic transfer shows the battle actually taking place, with, underneath the print, the inscription "The Young Alexander of France / May boast of his powers in vain / When Nelson appears tis confessed / That Britons are Lords of the main." This print appears on a variety of jugs and mugs, in a variety of ware. Perhaps the most flamboyant of all is of canary yellow pot, generally believed to have been produced at Swansea.

Next there is a very fine waist-length, oval portrait of Nelson, flanked by putti and topped by a scroll cartouche in which is inscribed "Admiral Lord Nelson" and which, in its turn, is surmounted by a coronet. Below this, in plan form, is set out the disposition and names of the ships at the battle, the plan being encaptioned in a ribbon cartouche "Battle of the Nile".

Lastly, there is a rather poorly executed transfer of Nelson, looking very fat-faced and, really, very unlike the admiral indeed. This is encaptioned "Lord Nelson" and the whole is set in a circular 'chain' cartouche. Below is set out the rhyme "Here's a health to brave Nelson, Old England's boast. The Hero of the Nile, Let this be our toast". This appears, in brown on a 23.75cm diameter plate and in black, overglaze enamelled, on a creamware jug 21.25cm high by 10.6cm diameter. This last also carries a transfer of Cornwallis and is encaptioned "Here's our old friend and success to the peacemakers", which means it was almost certainly published at the time of the Peace of Amiens.

That exhausts the known transfer pieces. There is, however, one tankard which, though at first sight looks transferred, is actually very finely and ingeniously freestyle painted. This piece is 14.35cm high by 9.35cm diameter, cream-ware, but of rather poor quality, black-rimmed to the top, with a boldly executed head-and-shoulders portrait of the admiral looking half to sinister, dressed in uniform and wearing cocked hat, set against a scene of a naval battle, the ships shown firing broadsides. Below, in a ribbon cartouche which is further ornamented by laurels, is the caption "Success to Adml Nelson". There is, of course, no absolute proof that this is intended to be the Battle of the Nile. But

156. This print of Nelson appears recorded on two pieces, this plate and a jug published for the Peace of Amiens. Since the rhyme expressly identifies Nelson as "Hero of the Nile", it may well have been first published in 1798 and reissued in 1802.

the pottery is absolutely 'right' for the date, and it is odd, if the battle is Trafalgar, that no mention is made of Nelson's death.

Just short of a year after the battle of the Nile Sir Sidney Smith successfully defended Acre against the assaults of Napoleon. There is a rather fine jug in the Willett collection commemorating this feat, showing the *Tiger* in full sail. Above, in a ribbon cartouche, is the caption "Success to Sr Sidney Smith"; and below the caption "Sr Sidney Smith Embarking on Board the Tiger of 74 Guns after Defeating Bonaparte at D'Acre" (as far as the authors can ascertain the *Tiger* did, in fact, carry 84 guns).

Nelson's next battle, Copenhagen (April the 2nd 1801), and his subsequent elevation to a viscountcy, were, curiously, almost entirely uncommemorated. The only known piece produced to mark the event was a very beautiful creamware (? Wedgwood, but it is unmarked) dinner service. Of this just a very few pieces survive. You can see some in the Nelson museum at Monmouth. A typical plate from the service is brown-edged, painted round the rim with a naturalistic wreath of oak leaves and acorns which is broken

155. At first sight this Nelson piece looks to be transfer-printed; but close examination shows that it is, in fact, very exactly free-style painted. Nevertheless it was produced as a multiple – two almost similar examples are recorded, one at Greenwich and one in the very spectacular Nelson McCarthy Collection at Portsmouth. The battle is almost certainly the Nile.

157. The only ceramic commemorative that records Copenhagen. It is part of what must have been a magnificent creamware dinner service. This is often catalogued as having belonged to Nelson: a doubtful claim.

top and bottom by two blue-painted ribbon cartouches, in which are, in brown, "Nelson the Glorious 1st of August", with just below in the body of the plate, "Aboukir" and, "Nelson the San Josef", with, on the body, "14th Feb". In the centre of the plate inside a green leaf cartouche, secured at the bottom by a blue bow, is a dominant brown anchor surrounded by the wording "Nelson 2nd April Baltic".

This service is usually catalogued as having belonged to Nelson. To the authors this seems unlikely. The decoration is very fine and very restrained. The effect of the whole piece is one of great, but quiet, elegance. Nelson was a total extravert. His tastes ran to flamboyant things, decorated in great profusion with his honours and arms. It seems totally out of character for either him or Lady Hamilton to have ordered such a service as this. It seems far more likely that the service was ordered by some admirer of Nelson, possibly by one of his captains, as a tribute to the Admiral, but for use by the buyer.

In the autumn of 1801 peace broke out. The Peace of Amiens, as it became known, was first mooted in preliminary discussion on October the 2nd. These preliminary talks dragged on for twenty days, and the cease-fire was declared official on October the 22nd. Once this happened talks restarted on the final terms of a lasting treaty. These negotiations took place at a higher level, between Lord Cornwallis and M. Talleyrand, at Amiens. The final treaty was not signed until March 1802.

The Peace of Amiens was celebrated by few, but particularly beautiful, pieces. These fall into two distinct classes:

The first is a series of tankards, made by the Bristol pottery in a number of differing sizes, but all identically decorated with a brown transfer, liberally and brilliantly enamelled in a polychrome palette, showing the female figures of peace and plenty, with the flags of England and of France, flanking a 'corinthian' pillar on which is inscribed "Peace signed at Amiens between England, France, Spain and Holland March 27 1802", the pillar topped by a wreath of leaves and the initials GR. The transfer includes the mark 'Bristol Pottery' together with a miniature view of the works.

The second is a series of underglaze printed jugs, potted variously in Liverpool and in Swansea, printed in either green or dark blue with a transfer running right round the piece and showing, against a background of Amiens, an elaborate allegory of peace in which Britannia sits, holding medallion portraits of "George III for ever" and "Down with Bonaparte" in a chariot drawn by a pair of crowned lions, on the back of one of which sits putti holding a flag entitled "Britons Rejoice" and above which floats a further cherub holding a scroll emblazoned "May Peace be restored", together with further figures of putti sporting on the grass in front of a female figure (Britannia?) who sits beneath a tree in which is perched the dove of peace, flanked by a beehive and heaped with the fruits of the soil. Around the neck of the jug is the caption "Britannia's triumph on the restoration of peace" – "Plenty attending the blessing of peace".

The peace ended on October the 18th 1803. Nearly two years later to the day, on Monday, October the 21st, Nelson kneeling at his desk because all the furniture had been taken away and the ship stripped for action ('Take care of my Guardian Angel', Nelson said, as they removed Emma's picture from the wall) writes in his journal: 'At daylight saw

158. A magnificent printed and enamelled Bristol pottery mug celebrating the Peace of Amiens in 1802. By courtesy of the City Art Gallery, Bristol.

159. This simple souvenir of Cornwallis may have been made at the time of Yorktown (1781) or even on his appointment to Ireland (1798). Or, of course, it may have been a production of 1802 and the Peace.

95

160. Another puzzle piece featuring Cornwallis: the caption reads "Marquis Cornwallis to whose clemency and bravery Ireland owes her Preservation". When it was made is uncertain: it could be celebrating His Lordship's tenure as Lord-Lieutenant of Ireland, or it could be a Peace piece, made for the Irish market. By courtesy of the City of Liverpool Museums.

161. A very fine blue-and-white bowl commemorating the death of Nelson. The portrait and the sentiment appear on various pieces, but the offset floral addition makes this a rare transfer.

the Enemy's combined Fleet from East to E.S.E. bore away; made the signal of Order for sailing and to prepare for Battle.'

Trafalgar was about to begin.

The battle commenced at ten minutes to midday, when the French fired at the *Royal Sovereign* (Collingwood). By half past four that afternoon it was over. Conquest, as Collingwood reported when he wrote 'there never was so complete an annihilation of a fleet', was overwhelming. Of the 33 ships in the Franco-Spanish fleet, 18 were captured, 4 surrendered within two weeks, and 11 reached Cadiz never to put to sea again; 20,000 prisoners were taken and 2,800 were dead (and British losses numbered only 429).

But Nelson was dead.

On December the 4th the *Victory* came into Portsmouth. On December the 23rd she finally anchored at Greenwich and Nelson's body, in an inner coffin made from the mainmast of *L'Orient*, the French flagship at the Nile, a lead shell, and an outer, elaborately silver-chased coffin, was carried ashore. From January the 5th Nelson lay in state in the Great Painted Chamber at Greenwich. Then, on the 8th, he was taken by river to the Admiralty. Here he lay overnight and the next day, in a triumphal car shaped like a ship on wheels (there are several very striking glass pictures of this 'funeral carriage'), he was drawn in final procession to St Paul's.

Ceramically few single events have been more lavishly celebrated than Trafalgar. Jugs, mugs, bowls, dinner services . . . potter after potter rushed to publish tributes to Britain's great hero. The great majority feature simply Lord Nelson and his by-then-famous signal. But a considerable variety were more ambitious and are elaborate in their tributes to both the battle and its victor. And one, at least, was published to raise money for a fund which was started to succour the widows and orphans of the great contest.

In detail, the Trafalgar transfers which are likely to be met with are:

(a) The Nelson Victories: an allegorical design of a pyramid and crocodiles (symbolizing the Nile), a fort (symbolizing Copenhagen) and an arrangement of militaria superimposed on which are two reversed flags carrying the word "Trafalgar" in a ribbon cartouche; the whole enclosed in a scallop shell. This also occurs as a moulded design, frequently coupled with a scene depicting the spirit of History and Britannia mourning at Nelson's tomb.

(b) A portrait of Nelson looking slightly to sinister, set against a background of the fleet at sea, contained within a circular cartouche in which is inscribed "England Expects Every Man to do his Duty", "Admiral Lord Nelson Copenhagen Nile 1798 Trafalgar", the whole surrounded by a quatrefoil cartouche of laurel wreaths in which are variously set the weapons and symbols of naval war, and the poem "Show me my country's foes / The Hero cry'd / He saw – He fought – He conquer'd / And he died" "Dear to his Country / Shall his memry live / But sorrow drowns the joy / His deeds should give." This is most often met with printed in blue and most commonly set on variously sized, and extremely well-potted, bowls.

(c) A very similar portrait of Nelson to (b) set within a circular cartouche in which is inscribed "England expects every man will do his duty" "Admr Ld Nelson" and surrounded by an elaborate design of flowing foliage. This is often combined with a transfer of the *Victory* with all sails set, within a simple wavy-line border inside which is inscribed "Victory", "Off Trafalgar Octr 21st 1805" the whole being set within an elaborate design of flowing foliage. These, or adaptations of these, are to be found on both mugs and jugs.

(d) A Sunderland pink-lustre series of varying-sized mugs and jugs on which are a black print, overglazed in a brilliant polychrome palette, showing a miniature head-and-shoulders portrait of Nelson looking to dexter, contained within an oval miniature cartouche, flanked by an elaborate surround of flags, ships and the angel of victory. Below, normally set into two 'blocks' is this verse headed "Trafalgar": "The Briton[s] mourn, what else can Britons do / While bleeding Nelson rises to her view / Still is there cause for triumph when she shows / The captured colours of our vanquished foes / And greater still when Fame was heard to say / All, all were Nelson's on that glorious day." This is a design which, like so many Sunderland prints, may well have been used long after the original date of issue. It is as well to take careful

162. Perhaps the most impressive creamware piece yet recorded for Trafalgar. The obverse carries an equally striking print. The jug is now in the Abrahams' Museum on Nevis, the island on which Nelson was married.

163. A very fine dinner service, printed in brown with orange decoration to the rim. The cartouche on the left represents Fame mourning at the tomb of Nelson.

97

164. One of the comparatively few commemorative frog mugs yet recorded: the mug is decorated with pink lustre and black-printed.

165. A very rare print of Britannia mourning the death of Nelson. This jug which is black-printed was almost certainly potted in Sunderland.

cognisance of the pot before deciding that the piece is definitely commemorative.

(e) A head-and-shoulders portrait of Nelson looking to dexter, with above the inscription "England Expects every man to do his duty" and below "Admiral Lord Nelson Born Septr 29th 1758, Died Octr 21st 1805 aged 47". This print is most commonly met with, printed in black, on creamware jugs and mugs.

(f) A plan of the battle of Trafalgar, encaptioned "Battle of Trafalgar" showing the geographic location of the battle and a crude representation of the lines of battle, together with a long, encaptioned, description of what took place.

(g) A variant of (f) encaptioned "Plan of the battle of Trafalgar", giving rather less geographic detail, but considerably more information on the exact formation of the lines of battle, and with a less detailed but still very adequate description of the event.

(h) (This is often coupled with (g). A list of the British ships involved, encaptioned "The order in which the ships of the British Squadrons attacked the combined fleets of France and Spain, Oct 21 1805".

On at least one mug there is an interesting combination of (e), (g), and (h) making one of the most comprehensive Trafalgar souvenirs it is possible to find.

(i) A very rare set of transfers, so far encountered only on an underglaze blue-printed bowl, probably Swansea, showing a fine portrait of Nelson looking slightly to sinister, inside an oval cartouche, encaptioned within the cartouche "England expects every man to do his duty" and below, "Shew me my Country's Foes the Hero cry'd. He saw – he fought – he conquered – and he died", the whole surrounded by an outer cartouche of militaria and oak leaves, with, to the right, an off-set design of thinly drawn flowers and leaves. This is combined with a print of the *Victory* firing her broadside, also set within an off-centred cartouche of flowers (but no leaves) and, below an arrangement of nautical emblems, Nelson's rank and orders set within an oval line cartouche.

(j) A very emaciated portrait of Nelson looking to dexter, set inside a circular double line cartouche resting on a swag of flags and naval emblems, in which is inscribed "England

166. The symbol on the side of this Trafalgar pot represents the three great battles of Nelson and appears, printed and moulded, on a wide variety of ware. Teapots are, as a class, amongst the rarer shapes of commemorative.

expects that every man will do his duty" and above which, outside the cartouche, is inscribed "Admiral Nelson" and below which "Victory".

This print is believed to be of Liverpool origin and certainly appears on jugs with the characteristic Herculaneum ribbed base.

(k) The transfer (j) also occurs on the one side of a very rare jug believed to have been published to help raise funds for the 'Patriotic Fund'. The other side of this jug carries a very finely printed scene of a widow and children in a garden, above which is the inscription "Behold the widow casting herself and orphans on benevolent Britons". (From the somewhat over-cheerful air of the children and the attitude of the widow it seems very likely that this was a stock decorative transfer, which with the addition of the apposite wording, the potter used to 'do a turn' when the jug was commissioned). The piece is further ornamented by a printed ovoid oak-leaf cartouche, in which is hand-lettered "A Hero great was he / His country's praise and pride / Most gloriously he fought / And for his country died". The prints on the jug are all most delightfully overglaze enamelled in blue, red and yellow.

(l) The same 'emaciated' portrait appears on another extremely rare jug, probably Herculaneum, which carries on its reverse side the rhyme "In Death's terrific icy arms / The

167. This print of Nelson, though usually less commanding in scale, is to be found on a wide variety of ware.

168. Quite often used on mugs and jugs as the obverse to 167, this transfer shows the plan of the battle of Trafalgar, with a good detailed description.

brave illustrious Nelson lies / He's free from care & war's alarms / Sees not our tears nor hears our sighs / Cold is the heart where valour reign'd / Mute is the tongue that joy inspir'd / Still is the arm that conquest gain'd / And dim the eye that glory fir'd". The jug is 15.6cm high, black-transferred and well potted.

(m) A very rare transfer seen so far only on a creamware (? Sunderland potted) jug, 21.25cm high, black-printed with an elaborate design of a sorrowing Britannia, backed by a tree in which is hung the Victor's crown, attended by the British Lion, with above, in a ribbon cartouche, the word "Trafalgar", and below, "Britannia leaning upon his Lordship's armorial ensigns, accompanied by her Lion protecting the Union shield and spear, mourns for the loss of her illustrious Hero Lord Nelson".

(n) A range of 'Portobello' jugs, which carry small medallion portraits of Nelson and the fleet, encaptioned "England expects every man to do his duty" "Adm Ld Nelson". These, once again, are a classic example of existing designs being quickly converted to meet a new need. The Nelson print has obviously been introduced into a space left fortunately empty by the chinoiserie design typical of this ware. The result, of course, looks hopelessly overcrowded; nor do Nelson and small chinese people in junks make happy jug fellows.

(o) A dryware wine-cooler, with a very finely moulded figure of Nelson against a background of oak leaves. Marked Davenport. There is a theory, which the authors have not been able to substantiate as fact, that such wine-coolers were ordered for, and used at, Merton.

(p) A transfer showing the weeping Britannia, holding a medallion portrait of the Admiral and attended by the British lion, sorrowing at Nelson's tomb. This, on a very rare red-printed jug, is coupled with a transfer of fame blowing her trumpet, ornamenting a long, epic poem entitled "Britannia's address on the Death of Lord Nelson".

(q) A pair of transfers so far met only on a massive creamware jug now in the famous Abrahams Museum at Morningstar on the Island of Nevis. The one shows, within an oval cartouche, Nelson lying dying on a curious semi-circular

100

sofa, surrounded by three attendants. Within the picture, but in a scroll cartouche, is set (above) "The Death of Admiral Lord Nelson off Cadiz, Oct 21st 1805" and (below) "Long as Trafalgar's rocky shore shall stand / Long as the ocean wash its bloody strand / Long as Th' Historian writes the faithful page / And fame shall hand it down from age to age / So long shall Britons to their children tell / How Nelson conquered and how Nelson fell." The other, within a similar cartouche, but topped with a design of naval emblems, shows an elaborate obelisk bearing Nelson's portrait, flanked by female mourners. A verse, set in a scroll cartouche, reads "Why droops Britannia, midst victorious cries / Why sunk in sorrow whilst they rend the skies / Why, when her sons triumphant ride the main / Writhes she in anguish on the rack of pain / Say for what cause the nation's inmost sigh / Why the big tear stands trembling in each eye / Yet say it not, for all too well is known – the Hero flown."

(r) A very finely potted 'Turner'-style jug, decorated in dark brown. The jug is decorated in the front with a bust of the admiral looking to sinister, contained within a circular dot cartouche, with, on a ribbon cartouche above, the inscription "Nelson and Victory", and round the neck the message "The wooden walls of old England".

(s) A print of the hero in an oval cartouche, flanked by an involved design of flags and guns, with, beyond these, the sorrowing figures of Britannia and of a British 'Jack Tar'. In an open line cartouche at the bottom of the oval is the inscription "Adl Lord Nelson" and below the print but contained within a curious framework of 'bricks' is the legend "Born Septr 26th 1758 Died Octr 21st 1805". This print has, so far, been seen only on a creamware frog mug 12.5cm high by 8.75cm diameter, black printed. The mug was almost certainly potted in Sunderland.

(t) There is also a set of blue-and-white ware – plates, dishes, tazzas etc. – decorated with an elaborate allegory of Father Neptune carrying someone off into the watery depths. Within the border is a small bust portrait of a man, which is usually claimed to be that of Nelson. Who made the set/s and whether they are, really, authentic Nelsonia, is not

169. Perhaps the most flamboyant piece made to mark the death of the Admiral: the body is in a vivid orange, and the print is transferred in silver. The allegory of Neptune appears, in differing forms, on a variety of ceramic commemoratives, and is a noted feature of the engravings on glass which were so abundantly made in 1806.

170. A typical cartoon print of the 1805 period; the fear of invasion led both the Staffordshire and Welsh potters to whistle in the dark with a considerable quantity of ware cartooning Napoleon.

known. But they have the one notable advantage of being a great deal cheaper than any other piece of Nelsonia, and so make a very good starting point for any would be Nelson collector.

Trafalgar saw the last British naval engagement, and so the last of naval commemorative wares, until towards the end of the war when there was a small amount published to celebrate certain Anglo-American naval happenings.

But, of course, it heralded a period of intense military activity in the peninsula and a very considerable quantity of ware produced to celebrate the successive battles and victories and ennoblements of Sir Arthur Wellesley to Duke of Wellington.

Wellesley first went to Portugal in the summer of 1808.

Once there, he won the battles of Rolica and Vimeiro; but his reputation was badly tarnished by the shameful Convention of Cintra and on October the 5th he returned to England, leaving Sir John Moore as commander-in-chief. In 1809 Moore died at Corunna.

There is, curiously, only one piece known to commemorate his death. This is a quite superb caneware teapot, modelled with an overall 'plaid' pattern, the lid finely topped by a bold thistle and the neck embellished with a design of the national flowers. On either side is a sharply modelled, oval, conche plaque: the one portrays the General collapsing into the arms of his fellow officers, while in the distance his army traverses the steep road to the cliffs; the other illustrates an allegorical study of Fame and History, the latter inscribing Moore's name on the tablets of Fame, the whole surrounded by the panoply of War.

Following Moore's death, Wellesley was reappointed to the command; and from this time on he fought the series of battles that have become known as the Peninsular Campaign. These are:

The Passage of the Douro, 10th–12th May 1809

The Battle of Talavera 27th–28th July 1809 (after this battle, on August the 26th, Wellesley was created Baron Douro of Wellesley and Viscount Wellington of Talavera.)

The Battle of Bussaco, 27th September 1810

The Battle of Fuentes D'Onoro, 3rd–5th May 1811

A jug issued to raise money for the fund set up to succour the widows and orphans of Trafalgar

Colour Plate 5

The unsuccessful siege of Badajoz and the Battle of Albuera, 16th May 1811

The Battle of Ciudad Rodrigo, 19th January 1812

(For this resounding success, honours were heaped on Wellington by both British and Spanish governments. The Regency of Spain created him a Grandee of Spain, with the title Duque de Ciudad Rodrigo. And on the 18th February, he was advanced in the British Peerage to the title of Earl of Wellington.)

The Battle of Badajoz, 6th April 1812

The Battle of Salamanca, 22nd July 1812 and the subsequent occupation of Madrid. (After this battle more orders and elevations came Wellington's way. Spain awarded him the Order of the Golden Fleece; and this order with its pendant sheep is, from now on, shown on almost every print of Wellington. And Britain elevated him to become Marquess of Wellington.)

The Battle of Vittoria, 21st June 1813. (At Vittoria Wellington captured a French marshal's baton. This he sent back to the Prince Regent. The Prince, in return, elevated the Marquess to the rank of field-marshal of the British Army, sending him a field-marshal's baton and gazetting the appointment on July the 3rd. This is relevant to certain moulded mugs and jugs.)

The Battle of Orthee, 27th February 1814

The Capitulation of Toulouse, 10th–11th April 1814

Once the war was over honours were strewn onto Wellington's breast like dew on the morning grass. On March the 4th the Prince Regent had granted him permission to wear the Grand Cross of the Imperial Order of Maria Teresa, the Grand Cross of the Imperial Russian Military Order of the Black Eagle, the Grand Cross of the Royal Swedish Military Order of the Sword. Now, on May the 3rd, he was made Marquess Douro and Duke of Wellington, and the next month presented with the tangible evidence of a nation's gratitude: four hundred thousand pounds voted by Parliament.

The amount of commemorative ware published during the five years of Wellington's Peninsular War was, surprisingly, quite limited. It breaks down into two distinct groups:

171. Possibly the rarest of all commemorative teapots. It is the only recorded item published to lament the death of Sir John Moore at Corunna, and this particular pot is the only example known to exist.

172. Pieces published to celebrate Wellington's various victories are surprisingly rare: this beautifully decorated plate lists 'Albuera', 'Vimiera' and 'Talavera' in the cartouches.

173. One of the more elaborate Wellington commemoratives: these jugs, which usually carry a print of Wellington at Vittoria on the obverse, are often decorated with silver lustre.

celebration of his victories, and acknowledgement of his various ennoblements.

It is difficult to pin down exactly when any piece of this Wellingtonia was made. All one can do is take into account the battles listed and titles granted to Wellington, and then, applying a degree of common sense, suggest that it is likely that such and such a piece was made after such and such an event. Reading from the start of the Peninsular War to the Peace of Paris, the following transfers or moulded pieces are known to the authors:

(a) A plate, 11.25cm diameter, blue-printed with a head-and-shoulders portrait of Wellington, bare-headed but in full military uniform, inside a circular cartouche, outside which is an elaborate scenic border, and, in regularly spaced 'resist' panels "Lord Wellington", "Albuera", "Vimiera", "Talavera".

(b) A very finely drawn head-and-shoulders portrait of Wellington in uniform but bareheaded, in an oval shape, surmounted by a victor's laurel wreath and surrounded by a most elaborate design of the weapons of war, a laurel wreath, flags etc. Under this is the legend "The Rt Hble Lord Visct

Wellington K.B. etc., Etc." This transfer has so far been seen only twice: once, as above and once with the print encaptioned "Duke of Wellington" – which aptly illustrates once again the danger of taking transfers too readily at their face value.

(c) A delicately moulded jug, with a curious and most unlike waist-length portrait of Wellington looking to dexter, decorated in a brilliant palette, and encaptioned in the moulding "Earl Wellington". These jugs are also, sometimes, silver-lustre decorated round the rim.

(d) A primitive-style transfer of Wellington on horseback, with outflung hand, against a background of a fort and a city. The Union Jack flies in the foreground and by the hooves of the horse are a grouping of spent cannon balls, a drum, a broken mortar and a bugle. Above the print is the legend "Marquis Wellington" and within the print the word "Salamanca".

This print has also been seen with the word Marquis erased and "Duke" substituted: another case of the potter having, one suspects, a plate in stock and altering it to fit

175. A rare transfer of Marquis Wellington at Salamanca. This same transfer has been seen with the word Salamanca deleted and the Marquis changed to Duke: a clear case of the potter making an existing transfer plate do a turn for a new situation.

changed circumstances.

(e) A rather roughly potted jug, 13.75cm high by 8.75cm diameter, trimmed with silver lustre at the neck and decorated with a transfer, printed in black, showing a bust of Wellington looking to sinister, dressed in classical Roman style and mounted on a ribbed plinth standing within an elaborate design of the symbols of war. The print is encaptioned, below the design, "Marquis Wellington".

(f) A transfer of a small drum marked 'G.R.' behind which are positioned a number of spears, swords, guns, halberds and two outfling flags. The one flag is encaptioned "Victory of Salamanca July 22 1812", the other "Madrid taken Augt 12 1812". This transfer has, so far, been seen only once, on a Swansea potted jug, 10.00cm high, brown printed with an ancillary decoration of wreathes and bunches of flowers.

(g) Moulded mugs and jugs in various sizes, obviously made by different potters; the quality varies sharply from some very crisply moulded pieces decorated round the rim with typical Castleford blue, to rough pot which hardly holds the design at all, to fine 'orange peel' pot with the design applique'd on. The pieces show, reading from the handle round: Wellington on horseback, with underneath the horse's hooves the word "Wellington"; a soldier waving his hat in his left hand and in his right a curious 'scarf' encaptioned "VITTORIA", and a soldier bowing as he tenders a stick-like object (presumably the captured French marshal's baton); an open treasure chest marked "plunder", standing under a grape vine; a captured gun being pulled by a soldier, while another soldier, standing atop it cheering, holds aloft a captured French eagle.

(h) A very beautiful black basalt tea-pot with a lion spout and a serpent handle, on the one side of which, in a moulded wreath of laurels, is incised the wording "India, Portugal & Spain. Vittoria 21st June 1813" and on the other an allegory of Britannia crowning a bust of Wellington with laurels while Fame sounds her trumpet, the whole surrounded by a line-and-swag cartouche under which is the single word "Wellington".

(i) A transfer of Wellington, with drawn sword, on a spirited, rearing horse, the print encaptioned "Field Marshal

176/177/178. A pair of beautifully printed
and very finely potted blue-and-white
mugs: the transfers of Lord Combermere
and of Lord Hill are identical – only the
name is changed. In both cases the obverse
carries the print of the Duke. By courtesy
of the City of Manchester Art Galleries,
The Thomas Greg Collection.

Wellington Vittoria".

(j) A transfer, often the reverse to (i) on jugs, some of which have silver-lustre decoration. In this, within a wide eliptical cartouche, is a decoration of a fort flying the Union Jack and an artillery piece, above which is a long caption detailing Wellington's achievements.

(k) On various pieces marked Dillwyn & Co, a transfer showing a bust portrait of Wellington supported by, on the one side, Britannia seated with shield, spear and lion and with, under her feet, the French standard and, on the other, the winged figure of Victory. This is usually teamed with two other transfers: the one, decorated with crossed flags, is inscribed "Albuera Almeida Rodrigo and Fuentes", the other, with similar decoration, "Badajos Vimiera Talavera Salamanca".

(l) A transfer very similar to (k) and also found on marked Welsh pieces, showing the fleet instead of Britannia and with Wellington's portrait flanked by the words "Vittoria" and "Madrid".

(m) A transfer very similar to (i), but set within an elaborately decorative cartouche and encaptioned within a flowing scroll "The Duke of Wellington".

The final peace treaty between the Allies and France was signed on May the 30th 1814, and dubbed the 'Peace of Paris'.

This peace was celebrated by rather less ware than had greeted the Peace of Amiens. As far as is known, neither Liverpool nor Swansea produced anything specific. But Bristol did: an almost exact duplicate of their Amiens tankard, the same pillar (although often rather more slender), the same flankers and the same top ornamentation. The piece is, however, encaptioned "Peace of Europe signed at Paris May 30 1814". And the French flag has, of course, reverted to the Fleurs-de-Lis.

There is also a very curious cup and saucer. These are porcelainous, and carry transfers seen only on this set. They are pink-printed and show putti at play. On the saucer a cupid in a conche chariot holds a small flag encaptioned "Louis XVIII", and the word "Peace" appears at the bottom of the transfer. On the cup, contained within a scroll, is the legend "Wellington for Ever". The whole set gives the impression of an existing design rather hastily adapted.

Thirdly there is a transfer so far seen only on a jug 11.25cm high by 7.5cm diameter, rather crudely potted and decorated round the neck with silver lustre. This, black-printed, shows the hands of England and France clasped in friendship, flanked by the Union Jack and Fleurs-de-Lis, each flag emerging from an ornate scroll decoration. Above this flies the dove of peace with a sprig of foliage in its beak. At the bottom of the transfer are an angel's head and wings. In between, contained therefore inside a very open cartouche, is the rhyme "Thank GOD for the blessing of Peace / England and France in unity be / May truth love and friendship increase / And Britons for ever be free."

Fourthly there is a transfer so far seen only on a creamware jug 17.5cm high by 12.5cm diameter, probably made in Sunderland, black printed and overglaze enamelled in a polychrome palette showing, in a circular cartouche, a well-defined portrait of the Duke of Wellington looking half sinister, encaptioned so above the cartouche, and flanked outside the cartouche by the figures of Britannia and of Peace so encaptioned, supported by flags and resting on a decoration of guns and military symbols.

Finally there is a number of Swansea pieces decorated with cartoon treatments of the defeat of the French and the return of Peace and Plenty.

Once peace was signed Wellington went back to France and on January the 24th of the next year left Paris to replace Lord Castlereagh as our representative at the Congress of Vienna.

There is one very rare piece which is believed to be of Wellington at the time of the Congress. This is a flask 17.5cm high, 4.00 cm of which is a tall thin neck, transfer-printed in brown with an involved motif of vine leaves and grapes, on the sides of which are two identical portraits of Wellington bare-headed, but in uniform, looking to sinister with the order of the golden fleece clearly discernible round his neck. This is flanked by the initials S.C.: upon the significance of which the authors can throw no light at all.

It was at the Congress of Vienna that Wellington received

179. This very fine black-printed cream-ware jug is a product of Liverpool's famous Herculaneum factory. The same portrait print is recorded with two inscriptions "The Rt Hble Lord Visct Wellington KB etc., etc.," and "Duke of Wellington". In both cases the obverse of the jug carries the Dixon Coat of Arms. By the courtesy of the City of Liverpool Museums.

the news that set Europe quaking in its boots again. Napoleon had fled from Elba, landed in France, deposed the fat and futile Louis and was once more 'l'Empereur'.

And so followed the Hundred Days, culminating, of course, in the Battle of Waterloo.

One might well think that this was a victory which, like Trafalgar, would bring in its wake a deluge of commemorative ware. But no. Maybe the nation was fed up with the whole war. Maybe the appalling poverty and unemployment that had followed the delights of the 1814 peace treaty had taken the gilt off the gingerbread of military conquest. Maybe reform was too much in the air. Whatever the reason, only one piece is currently known to have been produced, and this commemorates the famous meeting of Blucher and the Duke at the inn of la Belle Aliance.

The piece is a very finely potted small mug, 6.25cm high by 6.25cm diameter, decorated overall with a brilliant blue glaze on which are white moulded applique decorations of, on both sides, a head-and-shoulders portrait of Wellington contained within a circular cartouche and encaptioned beneath in a scroll, "Wellington" and on the front an elaborate design of cornucopias, with on a similar scroll the legend "La Belle Aliance". The mug is further decorated with a rim border of vine leaves.

And so the era ended. Napoleon sadly surrendered to Captain Maitland on board H.M.S. *Bellerophon* shortly after six o'clock on July the 15th; and three weeks later, on August the 7th, sailed to St Helena and his last unhappy six years. (He sailed, incidentally, in H.M.S. *Northumberland*: which, presumably, explains the mass of 'Northumberland 74' transfers that one finds printed on to untold quantities of Sunderland pink-lustre jugs, mugs, bowls and plaques.)

Once Waterloo was over and Napoleon was safely pent (he died on May the 5th 1821: 'Sire,' they told George IV, 'your greatest enemy is dead.' 'Is she, by God,' said George), Britain settled down to a long period of peace when only in India was there any large-scale military operation.

However, savage though the Indian wars were, no more military or naval commemorative pottery was published until the Crimea.

The root cause of this war was, inherently, the anachronistic weakness of the Turkish Ottoman Empire.

The direct cause was a demand that a Russian protectorate be established to safeguard the interests of Christians within the Turkish Dominions.

This Turkey refused and on October the 5th 1853 issued a formal declaration of war. On the 14th the combined fleets of England and France moved portentously into the Dardanelles.

All that winter the public clamoured for action. On February the 27th 1854 Britain's ultimatum was sent by Lord Clarendon to Count Nesselrode. On March the 24th it was refused, and four days later the Crimean war had begun.

The first significant British action in the war was the bombardment of Odessa on April the 22nd. It was a notable failure – as indeed was the whole war effort. Cholera and incompetence ravaged the Allied armies.

And so it was with neither a fit nor formidable force that Raglan faced his major task – the reduction of Sebastopol.

Disembarkation at Kalemita Bay began on the morning of September the 14th. By the evening of the 18th there were some 27,000 British, 30,000 French and 7,000 Turkish troops landed on the Crimean shore.

At daybreak the next day the army set out for Sebastopol, the French and Turkish armies forming the right wing, resting on the sea, the British troops with a screen of light cavalry on their inner flank, taking the left.

180. The only mug positively recorded to mark the battle of Waterloo: the symbol of the clasped hands and the caption "La Belle Aliance" refers to Blücher and the Duke's famous meeting on the battle-field.

The Battle of the Alma

Late that day, they met the Russian army under Prince Mentschikoff, strongly entrenched on the southern bank of the River Alma.

It was a formidable opposition. The narrow river was bounded on the south by precipitous cliffs of up to three hundred feet high. Mentschikoff had first an earthwork battery containing twelve guns; then another battery of twelve guns; then the Russian army; and finally, topping all, yet another twelve gun battery. His men were well rested and organized.

181. Two children's plates, perhaps made in Wales, commemorating Balaklava and Inkerman. The Charge of the Light Brigade is (curiously) a rare transfer. Balaklava is far more often commemorated by transfers of either the Chasseurs d'Afrique or the Heavy Cavalry.

At two o'clock the Allies began to cross the river. By four the battle was over. But what a shambles it had been!

'Lord Raglan', writes W. H. Russell, the special correspondent for *The Times*,

> gave orders for our whole line to advance. Up rose these serried masses, and passing through a fearful shower of round, case shot, and shell, they dashed into the Alma, and floundered through its waters, which were literally torn into foam by the deadly hail.
>
> Sir George Brown, conspicuous on a grey horse, rode in front of his Light Division urging them with voice and gesture. . . .

(In at least one transfer commemorating the battle, and which is usually on a jug, the luckless horse has clearly been shot from under him. Sir George is seen, standing by its side, waving his troops on with drawn sabre. Russell mentions this incident later in his report: 'Down went Sir George in a cloud of dust in front of the battery'.

Losses were fearful. But the Allies prevailed and the Russians fled to the south-east in considerable disarray. Had the Allies pushed on in hot pursuit the war might well have been over far sooner. But the ailing French Marshal St Arnaud insisted on time to recoup and regroup. And so it was not until the 23rd that they finally marched on towards Sebastopol. And not until October the 17th – three wickedly wasted weeks – that the bombardment commenced.

Meanwhile the Russians had been working like lunatics. They built the great Malakoff redoubt. They built the Redan redoubt. And between them and down to the sea they strung a mass of earthworks and gun-pits.

The Allies duly attempted to reduce these fortifications. The attempt was a total failure, with the result that a 'raiding' force, with no base for operations, no proper commissariat and, certainly, no plans to face the rigours of a Russian winter had, willy nilly, suddenly to become a siege force.

And the Russians were not slow both to realize this and to take action to exploit it.

The Battle of Balaklava

On October the 24th (only seven days after the unsuccessful bombardment and the realization that Sebastopol could not be taken by sudden storm) a large body of Russian infantry, supported by both cavalry and artillery, was discovered bivouacking in the valley through which ran the road from Odessa to Sebastopol.

At daybreak next morning the Russian cavalry surged into action. One body of them, about four hundred strong, charged down the slope on to the 93rd Highlanders. The remainder, some thousand strong, charged down towards the Heavy Brigade. (This action is to be found on certain pieces of commemorative ware, usually entitled 'the charge of the Scots Greys at Balaklava', or 'the charge of the Heavy Brigade'. The Russian charge was aimed at the camp of the Scots Greys and the Inniskilling Dragoon Guards). They were, with the help of the 1st Royals and the 4th and 5th Dragoon Guards, soundly routed.

Then followed what is surely the most futile and lauded epic of even this silly war: the charge of the Light Brigade. Whatever the reasons – and many are mooted – the Brigade

182. Two in a series of black-printed
mugs commemorating nearly all the
Crimean battles, including Kertch. This
last is uncaptioned, and can be identified
only by reference to its source in the
Illustrated London News.

'never-drew rein until they had broken through the entire
Russian army'.

But then, of course, they had either to stay there and be
shot to bits or to charge back again. At this moment General
Bosquet uttered his immortal comment, 'It is magnificent,
but it is not war,' and, more usefully, ordered a squadron
of his Chasseurs d'Afrique to silence one of the flanking
batteries and so cause a diversion.

There is a very splendid transfer showing a most spirited
charge of the Chasseurs with dead men and rearing horses
all over the place, which is often paired with the charge of
the Scots Greys.

One thing alone is certain. The whole affair was a bloody
fiasco.

The very next morning the Russians were at it again.
Russian infantry, supported by the guns of the fortress,
suddenly appeared on the heights above the Inkerman Valley,
and though the Allies quickly dispersed them the inherent
weakness of the position was undoubtedly made only too
clear.

The result of this was all too soon seen.

As day broke on Sunday, November the 5th, a body of over fifty thousand Russians suddenly appeared on the crest of the hill confronting the British 2nd Division.

The ensuing battle raged for seven hours. The carnage was almost unbelievable. There was no attempt at strategy nor even effective regimental command. It was 'a hand-to-hand fight carried out amid a dark and drizzling mist, so that our generals had very great difficulty in discovering what was going on, and the officers fought among the private soldiers with their swords and revolvers'.

Finally it was done.

The Russians withdrew, having lost, Lord Raglan estimated, nearly twenty thousand men.

And so in Russia the winter fell. At home the Government fell. Palmerston took office. A variety of commissions were dispatched to the Crimea to ginger the generals up a bit. The Czar boasted that Sebastopol would never be taken. The army grimly and silently sat it out.

And then, at daybreak on April the 2nd 1855, the second great bombardment began. This kept up for several days. It was largely ineffective. Canrobert resigned. General Pelissier took his place.

Almost immediately after the appointment of Pelissier a plan to send an expedition to take the fortress port of Kertch was reactivated. The expedition sailed on May the 22nd, and enjoyed great success. By the early autumn it had virtually cleared the Sea of Azoff of all Russian forces, and this with very few actions and very little loss of life.

One of the few actions in this area, and the only one to be commemorated, took place on September the 21st near Yenikale. The English forces engaged were two companies of the 10th Hussars under Captains Fitzclarence and Clarke, and two troops of the Chasseurs d'Afrique; they beat a large body of Cossacks, 'charging them repeatedly, and compelling them to retreat'. This took place after the main expedition had returned to Balaklava: a body of troops having been left at Kertch to prevent the reopening of the supply road to Sebastopol.

183. A typical, cheap, Crimean souvenir: Victoria and Napoleon and the slogan "May they ever be united" appear on innumerable Sunderland lustre mugs, jugs, plaques, and even jerries.

The Assault on Sebastopol

On June the 29th Raglan, sick with worry and with dysentery, died. All that summer the Allied sapping continued. On August the 16th the Russians, making one last attempt to halt this advance and break the siege, launched a huge attack on the French front at the River Tchernaya. Finally on September the 5th a terrific cannonade began, lasting without pause till noon on the 8th. Then, the plan was, the guns would suddenly quiet. The French would storm the Malakoff. And as soon as they had spiked the covering guns the British would rush the Redan.

Duly, at midday, the firing ceased. Twenty-five thousand French and five thousand Sardinians rushed the Malakoff, leapt the ditches, mounted the parapet and, after only fifteen minutes savage in-fighting, the redoubt was taken.

But the British failed with the Redan and equally, the French failed to take the Little Redan, the Bastion du Mal and the Central Bastion.

General Simpson, who had succeeded Lord Raglan, determined to make another attempt the next day.

But when the next day came there was nothing to attack. The loss of the Malakoff had made the south side of the town quite untenable. Knowing that this would be so, Prince Gorschakoff had made plans to withdraw his troops to the north side and the town was evacuated during the night, the Russians setting fire to the town and to the ships that remained in the harbour.

And so the siege ended.

And so, come the next spring, the war ended; the peace treaty being finally signed on March the 30th 1856.

Needless to say there was a very great deal of ware produced to commemorate the events of the war. Very roughly, this breaks down into two distinct groups: general pieces and pieces made to celebrate particular victories (though even here it is difficult to be entirely precise as to exactly what is being commemorated: all too often, since the battles crowded so close one upon the other, two transfers, of two different events, decorate the same piece of pottery.

116

184. Four very rare Crimean transfers encaptioned "Incidents of the war". So far this series of prints has been recorded printed only on these particular children's plates.

Group One: General

The main motifs of the Crimean War are:

(a) The crossed flags of England and of France and the legend "May they ever be united". This major symbol is often accompanied by a female and a male hand clasped in friendship (presumably Victoria's and Napoleon III's) and the names of one, two, or three of the major battles. There is often a victor's crown of laurels thrown in for good measure. And sometimes the additional slogan "God save the Queen, Vive L'Empereur".

(b) The heads of Victoria and of Napoleon, in classic style, usually contained within wreath cartouches and sometimes accompanied by the royal coat of arms and the Lion and Unicorn. Again, the legend "May they ever be united" is usually well to the fore.

(c) French and English soldiers and sailors shaking hands. They usually carry their appropriate flags and are often standing on the parapet of a fortress (presumably intended to symbolize Sebastopol). Again, the legend "May they ever be united" is usually employed.

These motifs appear, either singly or variously permuted, on plates, bowls, mugs, jugs, ewers, plaques and everything else the potters could think of, including Sunderland pink-lustre jerries. Much of the ware is black printed and overglaze clobbered, usually rather inexactly, and a very considerable amount is decorated with Sunderland lustre. If a piece has "May they ever be united" on it, it is virtually certain it is Crimean. The only time the authors have seen the slogan used in another context was on a miniature 'slip' decorated can celebrating America's entry into the Second World War.

(d) The other motif which occurs in various forms on moulded pieces, mostly jugs, shows aggressive British soldiers bayoneting a fallen Russian eagle. A particularly fine example of this (and perhaps the original fount of the idea) is in very precisely moulded green dry-ware and carries the impressed mark "published by E Ridgway and Abington, Hanley, August 1 1855".

(e) There is also a rare transfer with a very involved design consisting of the flags of England, France and of Turkey, carrying their appropriate battle honours, rising from a bank of flowers against which are the coats of arms of England and of France banded together by a scroll in which is the legend "The Union of England and France is strength". Below the design is the caption "May England forever such unity boast". So far this transfer has been seen only on a mug, printed in black.

(f) More precise, but still of general nature, are two

A Bristol pottery mug commemorating the Peace of Paris: a very similar one had been made in 1802

Colour Plate 6

transfers which very frequently occur together. These show
(1) the harbour of Sebastopol with ships of the Allied forces
lying off the town and the masts of the Russian fleet clearly
visible in the background, with the fortress and the hills
beyond stretching away into the distance. The print is
encaptioned "Sebastopol". (2) A very similar view of the
harbour at Odessa, again with ships of the fleet in the harbour
and with, in the immediate foreground a very easily identifiable obelisk set within a square of railing. The print is encaptioned "Odessa".

(g) The Royal Patriotic Jug. This jug is 19.35cm high by
10.6cm diameter, is black-printed, and, usually, further
ornamented with colour and with gilding. It shows on the
one side a widow grieving, surrounded by her children, with,
above, an 'angel' bearing a scroll encaptioned "Royal
Patriotic Fund" and on the other a group of wounded soldiers
in a battle scene. The jug is marked on the base, in a most
elaborate military cartouche "The Royal Patriotic Jug,
published by S Alcock & Co., Hill Pottery, Burslem January 1
1855." It is further marked "G Eyre, Desigt" and carries the
diamond date mark.

The purpose of the fund, as published in its first circular,
was 'the succouring, educating and relieving those who, by
the loss of their husbands and parents in battle, or by death
on active service in the present war, are unable to maintain
or to support themselves'.

(h) A very charming series of transfers, so far found only
on children's plates, all of which are entitled "Incidents of
the war" above the picture. These show:

A group of three sailors seated outside a building, one with
a crutch balanced across his left knee, the print entitled
"Wounded sailors from the Crimea".

A group of three soldiers, one of them kilted, returning
laden with food, the print entitled "Foraging party in the
Crimea".

A spirited action scene entitled "A fight in the trenches".

A group of sailors seated round a 'billy can' over a fire;
the print entitled "The Naval Brigade".

A group of soldiers reading missives from home; the print
entitled "Arrival of the post in the army before Sebastopol".

J

185. A rare transfer celebrating the end of the Crimean War. The print has been recorded only on these jugs, sometimes in black, sometimes in blue, but always produced by the firm of Methuen of Scotland.

A soldier seated outside an English cottage, with his wife by his side and his daughter on his knee, the print entitled "A convalescent from Inkerman".

Group Two: Individual Battles

Alma A transfer of a very spirited action in which a dismounted British officer is waving his men on to the attack. The print is encaptioned "General Sir George Brown at Alma". This print has so far been seen only on a rather well-printed jug, transferred in black.

Alma A line of Scottish troops being led into the attack by an officer waving an upraised sword, presumably Sir C. Campbell. The print is encaptioned "Battle of the Alma, charge of the Highlanders". This print has so far been seen only on a jug, black-printed and very likely issued in series with the Alma jug.

Balaklava A child's plate, with a moulded border of animals, overglaze-enamelled and very possibly potted in Swansea, transfer-printed in black and showing a wave of cavalry crashing through a line of guns (presumably the charge of the Light Brigade). The print has so far been found on both 15.00cm and 17.5cm diameter plates, but only on plates.

Balaklava A print of the Heavy Cavalry in action against Russian horse. In the foreground three British soldiers are riding over two fallen Russians, while a third Russian is in the act of falling dead. The print is entitled "Charge of the Scots Greys at Balaclava". This print is usually found, in black, on rather coarsely potted jugs, but it has also been recorded printed in brown. It is one of the more common specific prints, a great deal more often met with, curiously enough, than the more famous charge of the Light Brigade.

Balaklava A print of the Chasseurs d'Afrique in action. The French cavalry are shown making a very spirited attack on the Russian square. In the foreground are a dead horse and a fallen beast with a dead rider. The print is encaptioned "Charge of the Chasseurs d'Afrique at Balaclava".

Inkerman A child's plate, 17.5cm diameter, with a moulded animal border, clearly produced in series with the Balaklava plate, showing a party of soldiers advancing in file, the leader carrying the Union Jack. In the background, cavalry are galloping in charge. The print is simply entitled "Inkerman" and has so far been seen only on this sized plate.

Inkerman A print so far encountered only on a very finely transferred mug, printed in black, showing a most detailed picture of the battle in progress. The main distinguishing feature is a fallen soldier in the immediate foreground, who is discharging his firearm with a huge puff of smoke at a line of advancing infantry. The print is encaptioned inside a straight-rule box cartouche "Battle of Inkerman".

Tchernaya A child's plate with moulded animal border, in series with the 15.00cm diameter plate of Balaklava, showing a cavalry action in full swing, with a group of cavalry and a fallen horse in the immediate foreground. In the background can be distinguished a banner emblazoned with the French eagle. The print is entitled "Tchernaya".

The Malakoff A very finely detailed black print showing, in considerable detail, the redoubt being stormed. In the foreground a ladder is being used to cross one of the defence ditches. The print is usually found either on jugs or on loving cups. It is entitled "Storming the Malakhoff". It has, interestingly, appeared once on a frog mug; in the authors' experience, commemorative 'frog' pieces are rare.

The Redan In series with the print of the Malakoff is an equally finely printed transfer of the action at the Redan. It shows a very fierce hand-to-hand action taking place, and, whether by intent or not, gives the impression that things went rather better for the British than in fact they did.

Kertch There is a very rare mug, uncaptioned, 9.35cm high by 8.25cm diameter, black-printed and clearly made by the same factory that made the Inkerman mug, which illustrates the cavalry action of the 10th Hussars at Yenikale. The transfer, which runs right round the body of the piece, shows the Hussars at full charge, waved on by an officer with sword held high in his right hand (presumably either Captain Fitzclarence or Clarke). The Cossacks are shown retreating, and in the immediate foreground a Hussar is impaling a fleeing Russian on his sword. The print is taken from an illustration in the *Illustrated London News* of October the 27th.

Peace Curiously enough very little recorded ware seems to have been published for the Peace. Two pieces only are

186. An interesting little local souvenir: compare this with the George IV Coronation plate (plate 65) and the Victorian Coronation mug (plate 94). By courtesy of the Sheffield City Museum.

known to the authors:

(a) A jug, finely printed, showing on the one side British and French soldiers and sailors shaking hands at Sebastopol, while above floats the spirit of Peace holding laurel wreaths over their heads, the print being encaptioned, in a ribbon cartouche, "The brave soldiers and sailors of the Crimea"; and on the other a typically Victorian scene of one returning hero being rapturously greeted by his wife while another is more sedately welcomed by his stoutly respectable father. In the background the spirit of Peace holds a small ribbon cartouche on which is inscribed the single word "Peace". The jug is marked on the base in a cartouche of flags and of laurel wreaths "Peace" and "D. Methuen & Son". (David Methuen & Sons of the Kirkcaldy Pottery, Kirkcaldy, Fife, potted from the first half of the nineteenth century right up to the 1930s. Since this piece was made in Scotland it is odd that none of the soldiers shown was a Highlander.)

(b) A beaker inscribed, within a wide border of laurel leaves, "Peace Festival held at Worksop, May 29th 1856". This beaker was, presumably, used by children at the festival party and given to them at the end of the day (see the local plate published in Leeds for the coronation of George IV).

And so the war was over. But although 1856 saw the end of the Crimean War and the consequent end of Crimean commemoratives, the Victorian potters had but a very short time to wait before the next military event sent them scurrying back to their commemorative kilns.

The centenary of the Battle of Plassey, the battle that had added Bengal to the British Dominions, and so clinched the concept of the British Raj, fell on June the 23rd 1857. It was an event for celebration. And there were some rather handsome moulded jugs, which come in differing sizes, made especially to commemorate it. These are usually in white but occasionally have a very beautiful deep lavender glaze against which the moulded figures show up most effectively. The design shows Clive rallying his troops for the last assault, in an involved and highly stylized sequence from the nineteenth century's idea of an eighteenth century battle. (It is nearly always miscatalogued, often as a Crimean War piece, despite the fact that the soldiers are wearing uniforms that are clearly of the mid-seventeen hundreds.)

So it is ironic that it was just at this moment that England heard of the Indian Mutiny.

As far as is known none of the actions in the Mutiny were commemorated. But the two major heroes were: Sir Colin Campbell, but always in conjunction with General Sir Henry Havelock, and Havelock on his own. The three recorded pieces are:

(a) A jug, 15.6cm high by 9.35cm diameter, finely moulded with bust portraits set within open laurel wreaths, glaze-decorated in blue and embellished with copper lustre, showing on the one side Campbell in full military uniform but bareheaded and with his arms crossed, with the moulded caption beneath the figure "Sir C Campbell" and on the other Havelock in similar stance, but with his right hand holding his coat, the figure also encaptioned with his name.

(b) A very decorative jug, 20.00cm high by 8.75cm diameter with a finely moulded lion handle and a coat of arms at the spout, glazed on the body with a bright blue glaze against which is the white bust figure of General Havelock. A similar jug in white has the potter's mark Cockson & Hardings, and carries a diamond mark appropriate to Havelock's death on November the 25th 1857.

(c) A mug, 8.00cm high by 8.75cm diameter, printed in black with a rather mournful portrait of the general, the print encaptioned under the portrait "Sir Henry Havelock". (The reverse of the mug carries a print of Garibaldi; a clear case of an old print being resurrected to serve a new turn.)

And so, commemoratively speaking, there was peace. Except that 1859 was the year of the war that never was!

Europe was in a considerable state of ferment. Napoleon III in particular was being viewed with uneasy eyes.

There was talk of his uncle.

There was even talk of invasion.

It was against this background that in the spring of 1859 it was decided to re-raise the Volunteers. By the spring of 1860 over seventy thousand men had enrolled. Delighted with this manifest of her people's loyalty, the Queen decided to hold two great reviews. The first was on June the 23rd

187/188. Either side of a jug commemorating the military heroes of the Indian Mutiny. Sir Colin Campbell bears a curious resemblance to Napoleon III.

189. A very rare transfer of Sir Henry Havelock, probably made at the time of his death, in 1857.

1860, and was held in Hyde Park, when twenty thousand Volunteers paraded before their sovereign.

The second was held on August the 7th, in Edinburgh.

Coincidental with the Volunteers was the formation of the National Rifle Association, the Queen testifying her enthusiasm for this by firing the first shot at their initial meeting on July the 2nd on Wimbledon Common. They continued to meet at Wimbledon until 1889 when they transferred to Bisley, Doulton making a very attractive moulded stoneware jug to commemorate the final Wimbledon shoot.

There was quite a lot of Volunteer pottery produced.

The most important piece is a moulded jug, published by the Sandford Pottery and marked so on a moulded ribbon cartouche immediately under the registration mark. Of this pottery nothing is known. It does not appear in Mr Godden's most exhaustive *Encyclopaedia of Marks*, nor can any trace be found of it in any pottery records. The jug comes in a variety of sizes, but always with the same moulding.

The lip is moulded with the date 1860. In the centre is a finely modelled bust portrait of Queen Victoria looking to sinister, with her hair plaited into the distinctive 'bun and loop' style, the whole contained in a circular cartouche of laurel wreath topped by the crown. Under this in a ribbon cartouche is inscribed "Defenders of our Queen and Country". Flanking this central motif, as an overall frieze, are figures of a Soldier, a Sailor (they hold hands), an English and a Scottish Volunteer. And underneath them, in a running caption, is the wording "Our Army and Navy and Brave Volunteers". The jugs have a high inner-glaze, and are either of dry-ware or a rough-glazed light buff coloured pot. The registration mark is for September, which seems clearly to indicate that they were inspired by the royal reviews.

Another interesting jug is moulded, lustre-trimmed and underglaze-decorated in polychrome palette. It has a 'rifle' handle, topped by a lion, and shows on either side a Volunteer in the unmistakable peaked shako. It is uncaptioned.

Other pieces are: porcelainous cups and saucers printed (usually in a deep lavender) with two Volunteers on a rifle range, with a tented camp in the background. This is believed to be Wimbledon Common, where the 'shoots' took place.

The cups sometimes carry a further print of an emblematic arrangement of flags, cannons, drum, swords, cannon balls etc. The print is often inscribed "British Rifle Volunteers".

Small – 10.00cm diameter – plates, usually printed in blue, with "movements for rifle drill" on them. These were obviously produced as sets – probably with six to a set. They are uncaptioned.

Larger, 17.5cm diameter, plates, often printed in purple, showing various positions of combat between a swordsman and a man armed with rifle and bayonet. The illustrations on both these sized plates are based on illustrations from the 'Manual Exercise', a publication of the School of Musketry at Hythe, an establishment set up in 1857 for the particular training of officers and N.C.O.s.

And so the military century proceeded with a series of minor, but uncommemorated, wars until in 1884 'Chinese' Gordon was besieged in Khartoum. Gordon called home for reinforcements. The Government reminded him that his orders were to evacuate the city. But the country was on Gordon's side and, finally, Lord Wolseley with a relieving force started to ascend the Nile.

They were, of course, too late. On January the 26th 1885, after a total siege of 317 days, the town fell.

Gordon was lionized and immortalized by the potters, notably by Doulton who produced a series of jugs in his honour. History seems to be on the more sober side of Gladstone.

Of the last fifteen years little remains to be said. All was, commemoratively speaking, peace. Peace that was to go in 1899 and to leave the century floundering in the highly recorded wastes of the Boer War.

190. A typical late-Victorian product of the Doulton factory: this particular jug records the exploits of Stanley and the ill-fated expedition he led to relieve Emin Pasha in 1886.

191. Another Doulton jug: one of many pieces published to regret the death of Gordon at Khartoum.

192. The 1800 Act of Union with Ireland was commemorated by at least two transfers. It is thought that this slogan may be a reference to the already formidable Irish population of Liverpool. By the courtesy of the City of Manchester Art Galleries, the Thomas Greg Collection.

193. A very rare transfer, celebrating the act of Union, showing "Hibernia rejoicing in the freedom of extensive commerce". By courtesy of the City of Liverpool Museums.

4
Politics and Politicians

In 1780 Lord North was Prime Minister (and of him there is no recorded commemorative piece). But only for one year. In 1781 he resigned and the Whigs, under Lord Rockingham, returned to office. There is rumoured to be a bowl in existence which shows a portrait of Rockingham and is captioned something like "Success to L. Rockingham". But although the authors have met several people who know people who've seen this bowl, they've never actually met anyone who has himself seen it.

Indeed the whole close of the eighteenth century is very weak in ware commemorating either statesmen or their acts.

Of the former, the two overwhelmingly dominant figures are, of course, William Pitt, second son of the Great Commoner, and Charles James Fox.

Extraordinarily enough, during Pitt's whole career only one act was seen by the contemporary commemorative potters as sufficiently important to rate a publication: the Act of Union of June 1800.

To commemorate this at least two very interesting cream-ware jugs were made.

The first, which is now in the Liverpool Museum, is black-printed with, on the one side, Ireland seated as the spirit of Commerce, with above, in a radiant cartouche, the legend "Ye sons of Hibernia rejoice in the freedom of your extended commerce", and on the other Ireland, crowned and holding aloft the cap of Liberty.

The second, which is now in the Manchester Museum, is also black-printed, probably in Liverpool, with on the one side Ireland holding the cap of Liberty, seated by a harbour-side, and carrying a cornucopia on which is encaptioned, in a scroll, "Free Trade" and on the other, within an elaborate floral cartouche topped by a merchant vessel, the inscription "May I be freighted with Irish manufacture and discharged by the true sons of Hibernia". (This last may be a reference to the already substantial Irish population of Liverpool.)

There is nothing known to commemorate even Pitt's death on January the 23rd 1806. And his great rival, Fox, is scarcely more remembered. The only contemporary piece the authors have ever seen or heard of is a small plaque. This is round in shape, finely moulded with a portrait of the statesman, decorated overglaze in a polychrome palette and, within the moulding, encaptioned "C.J. Fox". This may well have been made at the time of his death, on September the 13th of the same year.

The only other piece of any kind is a plate, 20.00cm diameter, pink-lustre trimmed and with a small moulded portrait of Fox in the centre, encaptioned in a moulded scroll by the single word "Fox". The plate, which is extremely rare, is impressed 'Fell', and Thomas Fell of St Peter's Pottery, Newcastle-upon-Tyne, did not, according to Godden's Encyclopaedia start potting until 1817.

(Do not, incidentally, believe anyone who tells you that delft or early creamware pieces punning on 'Beware of the Fox', often with the animal shown, have anything to do with Charles James. The pun is on being *fox'd*, an eighteenth-century term for drunk.)

And so, commemoratively, the old century dies and the new starts: left over from the eighteenth and (just) political in classification is a very small number of pieces made to deride, rather than laud, the works and influence of Thomas Paine.

Paine's *Rights of Man* was the testament of the more radical eighteenth-century reformers.

Someone, some 'loyal' potter, probably in Liverpool, riposted with a jug and a mug. Both are of creamware. The jug is decorated with a full-length portrait encaptioned "Mr Thomas Paine, author of the rights of man", and, on the reverse, a political cartoon of swine. The mug, with a red transfer of Paine, has beneath it the following verses "Prithee Tom Paine, why wilt thou meddling be / In other's business which concerns not thee / For while thereon thow do'st extend thy cares / Thou do'st at home neglect thy own affairs. God save the King" and "observe the wicked and malicious man, projecting all the mischief that he can". Both of them are in the Willett collection, Brighton. Both,

194. The arrest of Sir Francis Burdett in in 1810, for contempt of the House, produced a spate of commemorative ware. This is the most usual of the portrait transfers. On jugs, it is often backed by a somewhat biased description of the event.

alas, must be classed in the 'unobtainable' category as far as today's collector is concerned.

For its first decade the new century lay commemoratively dormant. And then, in 1810, came the celebrated arrest of Sir Francis Burdett. Burdett, M.P. for Westminster and a noted radical firebrand was, on the order of the Speaker, 'arrested' for breach of privilege and lodged in the Tower until Parliament was prorogued a few weeks later. The affair caused a considerable furore and to celebrate his release, various commemorative pieces were published. The most common is a transfer, printed usually in black, but sometimes in red, which shows a head-and-shoulders portrait of Burdett, the statesman holding a scroll clearly marked "Magna Charta". This is set within an open laurel wreath and floral cartouche, within which, in a ribbon reserve, is encaptioned "Sir Francis Burdett Bart. M.P. The determined enemy of corruption & the constitutional friend of his sovereign".

This design is usually teamed with a very simple transfer. Set within a plain open laurel cartouche are the words "Sir Francis Burdett Bart M.P. committed to the Tower 6 April 1810 by the House of Commons for firmly and disinterestedly asserting the legal rights of the British people".

Another far rarer transfer, so far recorded only on an

11.25cm high frog mug, black-transferred, shows a much more detailed head-and-shoulder portrait of Burdett, trimmed to an oval shape, and with the outline of the oval maintained by the inscription, "Sir Francis Burdett, the indefatiguable champion of British freedom" . . . "Engraved by T. Robson for Phillips & Co Sunderland Pottery", the whole resting on an elaborate floral design as base.

And there is one very individual piece indeed, which is now in the Manchester Museum; a very finely potted mug, 8.5cm high by 9.5cm diameter, decorated in silver lustre with, between two swirling leaf cartouches the simple slogan "Burdett for ever".

One word of warning, however. Some Burdett pieces, while employing the original transfer, were almost certainly issued in or about 1832, the year of the Great Reform Bill.

The next political figure to emerge on the commemorative scene was Daniel O'Connell. O'Connell was the founder of the Roman Catholic Association and the prime campaigner for Catholic Emancipation, both in Ireland and in Britain.

The Association's first trial of strength with the establishment came in the 1826 Irish election, when it so successfully extended its influence on the 'forty-shilling' freeholders that they voted against their landlords and for the Association candidates. But these, of course, were all Protestant.

It was in 1828 that there came real success.

In January of that year Vesey Fitzgerald, M.P. for the County of Clare, having been made a minister, offered himself for re-election.

It should have been a formality. Fitzgerald was a wealthy Irish landlord, popular, with an excellent political record; and although, of course, a Protestant, he was a strong supporter of Roman Catholic claims.

Against him stood O'Connell. A Catholic. A man who could not take his seat even if elected. Which, of course, triumphantly he was.

O'Connell couldn't sit in the House. But to celebrate his election a number of pieces were made, probably in Staffordshire, and destined for the exultant Irish market.

The most prolific O'Connell ware is a salt-glazed gin flask.

195. A particularly rare Burdett piece, decorated in silver resist. By courtesy of the City of Manchester Art Galleries, the Thomas Greg Collection.

196. This very finely printed plate, transferred in blue, commemorates one of the most minor fighters for Catholic Emancipation, John (Jack) Lawless. A much more popular figure was, of course, Daniel O'Connell, Pieces made to commemorate his victory at the County of Clare bye election in 1828 are, however, rare: they include both transfer-printed jugs and salt-glazed gin flasks.

This comes in two sizes: an 18.00cm flask unmarked, and a 23.00cm flask marked 'Oldfield & Co'. Both are very similar in style to the flasks featuring the Whig leaders of 1832; and indeed, at first sight can too easily be dismissed as yet another Reform piece.

The only transfer so far recorded, which appears on a series of creamware jugs, often red-printed, shows a finely printed portrait of O'Connell encaptioned "Daniel O'Connel Esq M.P. for the county of Clare, the man of the people" and is usually teamed with a laudatory verse: a typical one, which occurs on an 11.88cm creamware jug, reads "Rejoice sons of Erin rejoice / You have no longer cause to despair / For the people with one unanimous voice / Have returned O'Connel for the County of Clare."

Apart from O'Connell, there is one other minor hero of Catholic Emancipation who for some reason found himself ceramically commemorated, John (Jack) Lawless, who was one of the leaders of the Catholic Association in Ireland.

Lawless appears on a very finely printed 25.00cm plate. The transfer is in blue and shows Lawless in profile to sinister, holding in his right hand a scroll entitled "40 shilling free-holders". Around the head of the portrait is the caption "John Lawless Esq., Civil & Religious Liberty", and underneath the print is the caption "Order of Liberation".

The 'forty shilling freeholders' referred to on the scroll were, of course, the small voters who, largely, made O'Connell's election possible.

The demand for Catholic Emancipation became even stronger after O'Connell's victory. And finally, on April the 13th 1829, the Catholic Emancipation Bill was passed by 213 votes to 109 – receiving the royal assent, albeit reluctantly, that very afternoon.

Another great cause of the early nineteenth century was the abolition of slavery. The trade itself had been abolished in 1806, thanks largely to the fervent efforts of William Wilberforce strongly supported by Henry Brougham.

Slavery, however, still went on. Indeed, the economy of the West Indies was thought to depend on it. But to an England brimming with Reform ardour, particularly to Brougham and his ilk, slavery could not remain an indefinite evil.

In 1822 the movement for the final removal of this blemish began. (It is in this later period that all the anti-slavery commemorative ware was made. As far as is known there was nothing produced to commemorate or publicize either Wilberforce's 1806 bill or Brougham's 1811 Felony Act.)

Curiously enough this movement was started by neither Brougham nor Wilberforce. It was a Liverpool Quaker, John Cropper, who organized the first Society for the Total Abolition of Slavery. And ironically enough its headquarters were in Liverpool, the city that founded its fortune on the Slave Trade. This Liverpool venture, however, soon stimulated the interest and activity of that old campaigner Zachary Macaulay; and on January the 13th 1823 he invited to his house William Smith, William Allen and Thomas Buxton (of Truman's Brewery), and according to Allen, they then and there 'laid the foundation of the London Society for the Abolition of Slavery in our Colonies'.

The Society's campaigns were long and fiercely fought – with Brougham a prime figure of the cause.

197. A rare anti-slavery transfer made during the campaign that led up to the final abolition. On the bottom is the precise inscription "Negro Emancipation: August 1st 1834". Any transfer which features negroes freed from their shackles is almost certainly part of this campaign: transfers featuring Uncle Tom and Eva, however, have nothing to do with it, and are the result of the much later commercial campaigns of Harriet Beecher Stowe.

Finally, on May the 14th 1833, Stanley, the Colonial Secretary, tabled in the House a motion of five points of action toward the abolition of slavery; and the bill was given the royal assent on August the 28th. (Tragically Wilberforce did not live to see his great dream realized: he died on July the 29th that year.)

By this Act slavery was to end, and emancipation to begin, on August the 1st 1834. But the slaves, although freed, were not to be given sudden and unsettling liberty. Instead, they were to become apprenticed to their former masters under the vital clause 3 'That all persons now slaves be entitled to be registered as apprenticed labourers, and to acquire thereby all the rights and privileges of freemen, subject to the restriction of labouring under conditions, and, for a time to be fixed by Parliament, for their present owners.'

Clause 3 was a good idea, but not entirely successful in practice; and the apprentice system was finally abolished, and the slaves set free, in 1835.

There was a fairly considerable amount of ware produced

198. Perhaps the most dramatic and yet sentimental of all the anti-slavery transfers produced: the rhyme reads "From Sun to Sun the Negro toils, No smiles reward his trusty care, And when the indignant mind recoils, His doom is whips and black despair". Presumably the pun was not intended. By courtesy of the City of Liverpool Museums.

in the name of anti-slavery; most of it, one suspects, for propaganda purposes.

Undoubtedly the largest individual 'thing' was a dinner-*cum*-supper service. This is decorated with brown almost sepia transfers and shows, variously, a mother and child slave under a group of palms and a single slave kneeling, holding a Bible, and is further decorated with appropriate texts.

It is incidentally assumed that certain small plates, all of which carry the single figure, are out of this one large set. This may of course not be true, and the small plates may be a separate production. But the evidence does seem to point the other way. They are definitely not children's plates. The standard of transferring and the colour match up to the larger pieces. And the pot is of a remarkably similar nature.

The most precise piece, commemoratively speaking, is a perfectly splendid jug. This is 11.88cm high by 8.13cm diameter, black-printed on both sides, with a group of joyous Negroes, the central figure of which is rapturously throwing away his chains. The neck is further ornamented by a small transfer design showing Britannia standing by as a kneeling white man cuts the chains off a negro slave. On the base of the jug, in a line cartouche, are the words "Negro Emancipation" and, outside, the date, "August 1st 1834".

The most dramatic piece is a small mug, 6.25cm high by 6.88cm diameter, printed in green, and showing, in a scene of tropic splendour, a white man lashing with fervour and a huge whip at a hapless Negro kneeling before him, chained hands reaching out in supplication. Beneath the print is the verse "From sun to sun the negro toils / No smiles reward his trusty care / And when the indignant mind recoils / His doom is whips and black despair". The whole scene is redolent of the worst excesses of Struwelpeter and very, very Victorian in its treatment.

Wilberforce himself, curiously enough, does not feature on a single contemporary piece, either by name or picture. But there is a very fine porcelainous loving-cup featuring a slave standing with broken chains and arms flung wide that has the word "Wilberforce" writ large in a triumphant cartouche above his head. This piece was published much later, however. The one example the authors have seen is dated 1870.

There must undoubtedly be other variants of the anti-slavery design still unrecorded. As a rough and ready guide, the collector can reasonably assume that any motif containing manacled slaves or slaves breaking their fetters is of this campaign.

What quite definitely is not an anti-slavery piece is anything to do with Uncle Tom, Little Eva, or any of the other characters from *Uncle Tom's Cabin*. These were produced either when Harriet Beecher Stowe visited England in 1853 to drum up interest in the sale of her book, or at the time of one or other of the various theatrical impressions of the tale performed in the London theatre.

And now, in this first half century of Reform one must go back to the start of the greatest reform of all: the agitations

A remarkably finely glazed jug featuring Cobden, and on the reverse, Peel: a publication of the anti-corn-law period

Colour Plate 7

and machinations that culminated in the Great Reform Bill of 1832, the most prolifically and imaginatively commemorated political event of nineteenth-century British history.

The call for Reform started back in the eighteenth century, with Fox and with Burke. During the Napoleonic war less was heard of it. But once the war was over Reform was soon on everyone's lips again. And not just on those of the 'common people'. In 1811 the Hampden Club, the most influential of all Reform societies, was founded, with no less a chairman than Sir Francis Burdett. By 1816 Hampden Clubs were established in a great many of the larger towns and even in some of the villages that surrounded them. And during the coming years, London and the provinces were to be infiltrated by a host of Political Unions (not to be confused with Trades Unions) all dedicated to the cause of a reformed Parliament.

By 1819 Reform meetings were being held constantly throughout the land. And on August the 6th one particular one took place at St Petersfield, Manchester.

That fateful Monday, between fifty and sixty thousand people marched to the meeting.

Samuel Bamford, who led a large Manchester contingent, reports: 'The meeting was indeed a tremendous one. Hunt mounted the husting; the music ceased. Mr Hunt, stepping towards the front of the stage, took off his white hat (he wore, always, a white top hat) and addressed the people.' At this point the magistrates did something remarkably silly. They ordered the Chief Constable to arrest Hunt. He, very reasonably, pointed out the impossibility of so doing. They then determined to use the military to enforce their decision. They had at their command two hundred Special Constables, the 15th Hussars, a troop of Horse Artillery with two guns, the 31st Regiment of Infantry, and between three and four hundred men of the Cheshire Yeomanry and forty members of the Manchester Yeomanry. It was the yeomanry that were commanded to make the arrest. At first they were received with cries of goodwill; then, 'waving their sabres over their heads they dashed forward and began cutting the people'. The dense mass of the crowd quickly split them, brought them to a standstill, and hemmed them in.

199. A very rare transfer commemorating Henry 'Orator' Hunt and the tragedy of Peterloo. Such pieces often have a verse on the reverse. This actually is a portrait of Hunt: many transfers encaptioned 'Hunt' are in fact American heroes of the 1812–15 war (see plate 201). By courtesy of the City of Manchester Art Galleries.

200. The obverse of the jug in plate 5. This very simplified transfer of the charge of the Manchester and Salford Yeoman Cavalry at St Peter's Fields occurs on both jugs and mugs.
By courtesy of the City of Manchester Art Galleries.

135

201. A rare jug produced in 1819 for the massacre of Peterloo. The man, although encaptioned 'Hunt and Liberty' is not in fact Hunt, but Commodore Bainbridge of the United States Navy. The potters often used prints of Americans as stand-ins for Hunt, presumably reckoning that as the originals had been made only for export no one would spot the impersonation.

At this moment, Mr Hulton, the chairman of the magistrates seems entirely to have lost his head. Seeing his yeomanry so trapped, he ordered the cavalry into action. In truth, both the yeomanry and more particularly the regular cavalry seem to have used the flat rather than the edge of their sabres. But still much damage was done. When the affray was over, Hunt was under arrest, eleven people had been killed and four hundred injured.

And that was Peterloo.

There were, not unnaturally, a number of pieces made to commemorate such a dramatic and dastardly event; and also to regret the trial and subsequent imprisonment of Orator Hunt.

Many of these set a real commemorative puzzle. There are occasions when it is indeed Hunt who is portrayed, with the appropriate encaptioned sentiments. But all too often the sentiments are Hunt, but the face is Bainbridge or Lawrence or some other 'Yankee' hero of the 1812–14 British-American war. Presumably, the potters used these old transfers as stand-ins for Hunt, thinking themselves safe in the knowledge that the originals had been made for export, and so would have almost certainly never have been seen in Britain. The only guidance the authors can give is to look for martial symbols and, in particular, for the American flag. If the portrait is surrounded by these, and looks as if it is something more to do with Waterloo than Peterloo, it is almost certain you've got an American by the transferred tail.

The major Hunt pieces are:

(a) A simple transfer showing Hunt in a military setting (actually Lawrence) surmounted by the caption "Henry Hunt Esq." and with, beneath the print, the slogan "None of your butchering magistrates". This is recorded on only two pieces – a porcelainous jug further embellished with moulded floral decoration, and a pottery jug with no nomenclature but beneath the print the slogan "The great champion of Reform".

(b) A very similar portrait transfer to (a) (actually Bainbridge) surmounted by the caption "Hunt and Liberty". This is, on one creamware jug, further embellished with a ribbon cartouche set beneath the portrait print containing the slogan "May truth and justice prevail over injustice and Oppression".

(c) Various rhymes:

"The man who laughed to see an ass / Mumbling to make the cross-grain'd thistles pass / Might laugh again to see a jury chaw / The prickles of unpalatable law."

"Henry Hunt that pillar Bright / The father of the poor / Kind heaven will protect / And from illness keep secure."

Both of these were probably published at the time of Hunt's imprisonment, rather than immediately after Peterloo. (The fear of gaol sickness was a very real cause for alarm in the early years of the nineteenth century.)

There is, however, one further rhyme which is more certainly directly applicable to Peterloo. This is set within a circular floral cartouche, and headed "Truth and Liberty". It then reads:

"While mad oppression fills the land / Arise and claim your charter / Nor ever lend a willing hand / Your liberties to barter / United who shall dare oppose / A cause so grate and glorious / Exert your voices o'erwhelm your foes / Till Britons are victorious / And ever patriot's song shall be / In praise of Truth and Liberty."

There are then a number of transfers which are directly Peterloo rather than Hunt (and which in many instances appear on pieces as the obverse to a Hunt print). These are:

(a) A transfer showing in stylized form the cavalry riding over the fallen victims at Peterloo; across the sprawled victims is stretched a banner, bearing the caption "Murder". Below the print is the following rhyme: "The scripture crys out life for life / And God ordained it so / We'll not forget to pay the debt / Incurr'd at Peterloo".

(b) An elaborate design showing the weeping Britannia carrying a flag on which is inscribed "Hunt and Liberty" and sitting by the side of a tomb encaptioned "To the memory of the unfortunate sufferers at Manchester". Below the tomb, in a scroll, is the inscription "A bill of rights". Above, in a circular cartouche, is a small portrait of Hunt, entitled "Henry Hunt Esq.", flanked by a flag on which is written "No corn laws". To the side, opposite Britannia, is a further portrait, of T. J. Wooler, so encaptioned, with below this,

202. This Peterloo transfer is particularly interesting because it includes the only mention of Wooler and his radical publication *The Black Dwarf*. It has been recorded printed only on this one jug.

203/204. Two of the rarest of all transfers connected with Peterloo. The source of the prints is a Reformist pamphlet, issued in 1819 and entitled "The Political House that Jack Built".

a scroll reading "Black Dwarf": the radical news-sheet that Wooler edited.

(c) A spirited print of a single cavalryman with upswung sabre riding down a female figure. The woman is clutching a flag on which is inscribed "Liberty or Death". Trampled under the hooves of the galloping horse are further banners, reading "No Corn Laws" and "Hunt and Liberty". Above the pictorial print is the caption "Murdered on the plains of Peterloo" and, below, "Manchester 16 August".

(d) A print showing a pair of clasped hands set in front of the cap of Liberty arranged with crossed flags, the last emblazoned with the slogans "No corn bill": "The bill of rights": "A free press": "The . . . [too smudged to read] . . . of liberty". Below this is a rhyme: "O liberty! Thou choicest treasure / Seat of virtue! Source of pleasure / Life without thee knows no blessing / No endearment worth caressing". And under all is set an elaborate arrangement of scrolls with the slogan "A long pull, A Strong pull, And pull together, To retain our Rights". This has so far been recorded only on one jug, 10.63cm high by 6.88cm diameter, lustre decorated in pink, printed in black.

(e) A pair of prints taken from a Reformist pamphlet published in 1819, entitled 'The Political House that Jack Built'. These have been seen only on a pair of octagonal plates, 18.25cm diameter, printed in a rather muddy mauve, the one showing three battered victims seated on a hillock in the foreground, while Peterloo proceeds in the background, encaptioned "What man seeing this, and having human feelings, does not blush, and hang his head to think himself a man?" the other showing a conversation group of Sidmouth, Castlereagh and Canning, encaptioned "Dream after dream ensues; and still they dream that they shall still succeed and still are disappointed". The original print is also labelled "The Guilty Trio". The plates are further embellished with daisy borders.

There is also one Hunt piece which, although authentic Hunt, has nothing to do with Peterloo. This, the very rare print known as the Preston Cock, was published as part of the propaganda for the 1832 Reform movement and refers to Hunt's position as M.P. for Preston. It is a very graphic

05. A very unusual transfer celebrating the passing of the Reform Bill. On the back of the jug is an extremely rare verse which was, later, connected with the Tolpuddle Martyrs.

and highly spiteful cartoon print, featuring in rural roles Wellington, Peel, and other assorted Tory ministers, luring the Cockerel Hunt with a handful of golden grain. The whole print is encaptioned "Insnaring the Preston Cock – a Barn-yard scene". So far this print has been recorded only on jugs, black printed and overglaze enamelled with precision.

All the way through the next decade the call for Reform got louder and louder, and the country suffered greater and greater unrest.

In 1830 William IV ascended the throne (there is quite a selection of salt-glaze gin flasks modelled as William IV and impressed with the wording the "True Spirit of Reform". Many of these were probably made in 1832 – but it is very likely that the first were published to celebrate William's Coronation, in 1831, and were issued by the various Political Unions as propaganda for their cause).

On March the 1st 1831 Grey's new Government introduced the long-awaited Reform Bill, the privilege of presenting it to the House being given to Lord John Russell. And it was carried, but by only one vote.

The margin was too slender. The Government resigned. And a General Election was declared.

When the new Parliament met in June, Grey's party was strong as never before. With this new strength, the bill was pushed through the lower House and carried by fifty-five votes. And on the evening of the 22nd it was taken to the Upper House by Lords Althorp and John Russell. On October the 3rd Earl Grey rose to present it.

Four days later, the Lords threw it out. (It is interesting that every bishop but two voted against it: hence, of course, the slighting allusions to the clergy on various commemorative items.)

Nothing daunted, Lord John introduced a new bill, and this finally passed the House *without a division*, on Friday, March the 23rd 1832.

The following Monday it went to the Lords. Wellington once again announced his unequivocal opposition. 'It is not reform,' he said, 'but revolution.' And sure enough, the Lords rejected it.

The Cabinet now met to consider their position. Either

206/207. Either side of a remarkable jug, published during the 1832 Reform period, and featuring Orator Hunt in his capacity as MP for Preston. These jugs, which are printed in black and precisely overglaze clobbered, must presumably have been purely a local production. By courtesy of the Harris Museum and Art Gallery, Preston.

208. A fine and quite rare gin flask: other Reform flasks feature Brougham, Grey and Russell, but never, as far as is known, Althorp.

they must resign or the King must create sufficient new and reform-minded peers to carry the bill through the Lords.

This latter William was most reluctant to do. And he accepted the Government's resignation.

But even Wellington could not form a tenable Tory Government and William, on his advice, then wrote to Lord Grey requesting him to resume the Government of the country. Grey and Brougham waited on the King and told him they could do so only if they had the power to create peers.

With, it is reported, a surly ill-grace, the King agreed, and he also requested the Tory peers to withdraw their opposition.

And so on June the 4th, the bill was finally read and passed, by a majority of eighty-four.

The news of the final passage, and ultimate passing, of the bill was received nation-wide with fantastic jubilation, and a spate of commemorative ware in a quantity to match the nation's enthusiasm and swelling wallet.

(Indeed, second to the Diamond Jubilee, the 1832 bill is perhaps the most, and most variedly, commemorated event in nineteenth-century British history).

Transfers of the four main heroes of the bill, Althorp, Brougham, Grey and Russell, and of certain celebratory motifs, appear on a mass of different mugs, jugs and bowls, though seldom on plates, in a myriad different permutations. Listed here are the more important *transfers*; only when one is believed to have particular relevance to a factory or publisher is any attempt made to describe individual *pieces*.

(a) A cartoon scene in which King William addresses a startled House of Lords. In speech balloon he says: "My Lords and Gentlemen I have been induced to resort to this measure for the purpose of ascertaining the sense of my people in the way in which it can be most constitutionally and authentically expressed." This improbable scene is labelled "Dissolution of Parliament".

(b) Grey, Russell, Brougham and Althorp standing in a group. Grey and Brougham are holding aloft a scroll headed 'Pro Rege Lege Grege' which lists the names "Grey, Brougham, Russell, Althorp, Burdett, Norfolk . . . and many more good fellows Huzza". In a cartoon cartouche balloon,

Grey says "We are for our King and the people. The Bill the whole Bill and nothing but the Bill." On an anchor which is resting to the side of Lord Grey is an entwined scroll reading "God save King William". With its reference to the Duke of Norfolk, this transfer was probably published for the Hampden clubs.

(c) A stone pillar, on the base of which is written "King and Constitution" and on the body of which, in script, is emblazoned "Disfranchise stone walls and Parks give members to the people". This slogan is headed by the single word "Reform". On the pillar stands Althorp holding aloft a scintillating torch encaptioned "Truth".

(d) Clasped hands, often within a circular laurel wreath cartouche. In this context, this is the symbol not of the friendly societies nor of the trades unions, though both also employ it, but of the political unions which were prevalent in almost all big towns.

(e) An elaborate design in which the British lion lies in front of two pillars. These are marked, respectively, "Lords" and "Commons" with, on the base of the columns "Majority 84", "Majority 116". Above is the State crown, radiating brilliance, with the scales of justice arranged below. Overall is the caption, enclosing the design in a semi-ovoid frame, "The purity of the constitution restored".

(f) An arrangement of four, linked, circular medallion cartouches in which are named portraits of the four reformers. Linking the medallions into a composite ovoid design are the words, "The zealous and successful promoters of Reform". This transfer often appears on jugs potted in Swansea.

(g) Extremely finely printed portraits, and encaptioned so, of "Lord John Russell", "Baron Brougham and Vaux", "Earl Grey". The prints of Brougham and of Grey are sometimes signed 'Kennedy', and it seems a fair assumption that this extremely talented Burslem engraver did, in fact, produce all of these portraits.

(h) A very fine design showing Britannia, flanked by the naval ensign marked with the word "Reform" and the cornucopia of plenty, treading underfoot the broken gun of war, and spearing, with a staff topped by the cap of liberty, the writhing devil of Jacobinism. She is watched by the

209. A common Reform transfer: it shows the very unlikely scene of William IV threatening to dissolve parliament. In fact, William was far from ardent for reform. This print is usually found on jugs, but occasionally is also featured on impressive Reform punch-bowls.

210. A typical Reform transfer, usually found red- or purple-printed on jugs: with its reference to 'Norfolk', it is probably a production of the Hampden Clubs.

211. A very fine matched pair of Reform mugs. The one on the left contains the jacobin devil impaled on Britannia's staff, in the one on the right he is missing. The authors have a theory that this may be a print of the immediately post-Napoleonic-war period, revived and adapted.

212. Found on both mugs and jugs this features the Whig leaders laying the axe of Reform to the Rotten Borough System, which is most energetically defended by the Tory Cabinet.

British lion couchant who is, in his turn, flanked by the ensign and by a white flag marked "Union". In the distance is a sailing ship in full rig, representing the benefits of trade. Sometimes this print has, curiously, the prone Jacobin figure missing. The authors have a theory that this transfer was originally produced just after the end of the Anglo-French war (hence the reference to trade and to the Jacobin devil) and re-issued, or even possibly re-designed, at a later date as part of the 1832 campaign.

(i) Within an elaborate, decorative, rectangular cartouche the rhyme "Confound the Bishoprics / Frustrate their knavish tricks / On BILL our hopes we fix / God save the King!". This, clearly referring to the special opposition of the Lords Spiritual, certainly contains one of the most horrific commemorative puns ever perpetrated. So far this transfer has been found only on a 15.00cm diameter octagonal plate, printed in black.

(j) A 'primitive' portrait of Russell, his lordship looking to sinister and slightly downwards. The print is encaptioned "Lord John Russell". So far this print has been seen only on a mug, 6.88cm high by 7.5cm diameter, printed in purple, the obverse side of which carries the usual 'Kennedy' portrait of Brougham.

144

(k) Perhaps the most delightful Reform transfer of all. On the one side William and Adelaide stand, he waving his hat in his right hand, above them the State crown and the caption "Constitution Hill". To their left stand two (unidentified) figures, also waving; perhaps representing 'the populace', and to their right, in the far distance, a further huzzaing figure. On the other is an elaborate tree, upon whose branches are a considerable number of birds' nests, filled with hungry birds. The tree is hung with placards reading "Rotten Borough System" and "You take our lives when you take away the means whereby we live", and is encaptioned "The old Rotten Tree". On the one side of the tree Grey, Althorp, Russell and Brougham lay the axe of Reform to the roots of the rotten borough system, while on the other the Tory 'cabinet', Wellington, Peel etc., endeavour to prop up the tree against the Whig assault.

Finally, there is a considerable number of similar but different transfers featuring the Crown, the Royal Flowers and the word 'Reform'. These are usually seen in conjunction with one or more of the major transfers.

It is worth noting that while, of course, many of these Reform pieces are printed in black, a considerable number are printed in purple or lilac. Obviously this was a fashionable colour of the times; a fair number of William IV coronation pieces are in the same colour. It seems however to have enjoyed only a short-lived favour. By the time Victoria was crowned, although purple still had its place, it had been relegated to a more minor role, and by the time of her marriage, in 1840, it had slipped even further back in the popularity stakes.

While on the subject of Reform: there are also at least two pieces which feature one of the great Reform heroes and yet have nothing to do with the bill.

One is a very spectacular plate, 13.13cm diameter, with a moulded flower border decorated underglaze in yellow, green and blue and with, in the central body of the plate, a crisply moulded figure of the statesman, decorated in blue and yellow, with the moulded inscription "H Brougham Esq M.P."

213. A rare lustre-decorated plaque; it features William as "the only Royal Reformer since Alfred". This seems a somewhat obscure and doubtful claim to fame.

214. This transfer of Kinloch appears both on plaques and on very fine black-printed mugs. Kinloch is interesting as the only Scottish Reformer known to be commemorated.

215. An extremely rare mug black printed with a long and laudatory inscription to Henry Brougham. This mug, presumably, was published before he was raised to the peerage in 1830.

The other is the jug, referred to on page 39, decorated in polychrome palette with a moulded decoration showing the statesman set in a circular-rimmed panel surrounded by wreaths of flowers. Around the neck of the jug, which has a mask lip, is the impressed captioned "H Brougham Esq M.P." (The reverse of the piece features Denman.)

Both these pieces were, presumably, produced in or about 1820, when Brougham and Denman were two of the leading figures in the drama of the Bill of Pains and Penalties.

There is also a wide range of stoneware flasks featuring Grey, Brougham and Russell (although the writers know of none featuring Althorp), with such slogans as "The true Spirit of Reform", "The Peoples Right", "The Second Magna Charta". The two most featured manufacturers were Doulton and Watts of Lambeth, and the Belper Pottery, run by Joseph Bourne. Both these potters marked their pieces with impressed names and factories and the flasks frequently also have impressed on them the name of the ale house or spirit seller for whom they were made.

Apart from the big Whigs, another commemorated reformer was George Kinloch. Kinloch of Kinloch, J.P., presided at a Radical meeting in Dundee on November the 10th 1819, in the course of which he waxed somewhat forceful on the subject of Peterloo.

This speech was reported in full. And Kinloch was arraigned for publishing a seditious libel. Sensibly, and knowing he had absolutely no chance of acquittal, he fled the country on December the 22nd 1819.

A plaque and a mug were issued to commemorate Kinloch. Not his speech, but his election to the seat of Dundee in the reformed House of Commons, on, appropriately enough, December the 22nd. The plaque and the mug are both decorated with a portrait of Kinloch and this inspiring inscription: "On the 22nd December 1819, forced to flee his country and proclaimed an outlaw for having advocated the cause of the people and the necessity of Reform. On 22nd December 1832 proclaimed the chosen representative of the town of Dundee in the Reform House of Commons."

And so to the Corn Laws, Free Trade, and, after the 1832

Reform Bill, the greatest political commemorative splurge of the century.

The Corn Laws, and hence the tariff on trade, had been introduced in 1815. This because, after the war, it was thought necessary to bolster up home agriculture against the import of foreign grain.

This meant, of course, that over the years not only did food become very expensive but business generally slumped disastrously; many of Britain's best overseas customers, being big wheat-producing countries, showed marked reluctance to trade with a nation that would not buy their grain.

Finally, in 1838, in Manchester, Richard Cobden and John Bright and five others formed the Anti-Corn-Law-Association.

The fight had begun.

Over the next seven years the 'League' as it had become known, worked prodigiously: over two thousand lectures were delivered, four million tracts printed and distributed.

Then, in 1845, came disaster.

The harvest was the worst for years. And in Ireland the potato crop, blighted by disease, failed almost completely.

Faced with a powerful alliance of the Whig party and the League, Sir Robert Peel, on January the 19th 1846, presented the case for repeal. After strenuous debate and attack (mainly from Disraeli, who established himself here and now as the leader of the right-wing Conservatives) the bill finally received the Royal Assent on July the 26th.

The Corn Laws, and the League, produced a very great deal of ware. And yet, despite its quantity, there were comparatively speaking, surprisingly few variations of transfer.

(a) An elaborate design of a port scene, superimposed on which is an arrangement of the Royal Flowers surrounding a lyre-shaped cartouche in which is a sheaf of wheat, a sickle and a thresher. To the one side of this is a collection of agricultural implements, and threading its way through the top of the design, contained within a ribbon cartouche, is the slogan "Our bread untaxed, our commerce free".

(b) A different port scene, with in the foreground an arrangement of sacks and cornucopia. The sacks are variously marked "corn" and "cheap corn". From the mast of a vessel in the background fly two banners, reading, respectively,

216/217. A very rare moulded jug the one side of which features Brougham, the other Denman. This was, presumably, published in 1820 when Brougham and Denman were both legal advisers to Queen Caroline.

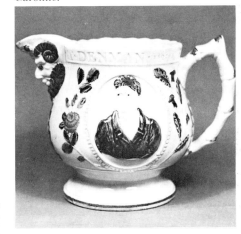

147

218/219. Either side of a beautifully made mug, printed with two unusual portraits of Russell and of Brougham. By courtesy of the Harris Museum and Art Gallery, Preston.

220. Another rather rare portrait of Russell: just visible at the top right is the political union symbol of clasped hands – a legacy from the 18th-century friendly societies.

221. A very unusual Reform rhyme, which amongst its other charms includes perhaps the worst commemorative pun ever perpetrated. All but two Bishops voted against this Bill.

222. A lustre-decorated jug, but possibly made in Staffs rather than Sunderland, decorated with a most unusual transfer. It looks far more the product of a local bye-election than any other reform transfer so far recorded.

223. The most common of all the free-trade transfers: these are usually found on either octagonal or round children's plates, black-printed and overglaze-clobbered. The same transfer is also often seen on small rather squat jugs, usually printed in black but sometimes in brown.

224. Compare the ship on this childrens' plate with the one in plate 225. The concept of a sail emblazoned with the slogan was a popular one of the time, but this vessel carries both steam and sail, an interesting nautical development that is, perhaps, most famously commemorated in prints of Brunel's *Great Eastern*.

225. An unusual print published by the Anti-Corn-Law League: this particular mug is of peculiar interest because it has a frog in it. Commemorative frog mugs are rare.

226. Another unusual transfer recommending the repeal of the Corn Laws and the cause of free trade: this is printed in blue on this very impressive loving cup, and is the only example of the transfer so far recorded.

"No monopoly" and "Free Trade". In the immediate foreground several mice are nibbling holes in a tract encaptioned "corn law".

Both these transfers may be printed in brown or black, and both are usually overglaze-'clobbered' in a fairly vivid palette.

(c) A very much rarer transfer, so far encountered only on a 13.75cm plate, printed in black and overglaze-enamelled, shows a ship just breaking out her sails as she leaves harbour; a pile of cargo stands on the harbour wall. Above, the print is encaptioned, "Commerce"; and below, "The Staffordshire potteries and free trade with all the world".

(d) Another rare print, again only met with so far on a plate, 15.00cm diameter, black-printed and overglaze-clobbered, shows a ship sailing into harbour, its sails embellished with the slogan "Free Trade". The print is encaptioned, over the scene, "Free trade with all nations".

(e) A print very similar to the last described shows an apparently identical ship entering a harbour, with in the foreground, a warehouse into which a number of barrels of flour are being loaded. The print is encaptioned "Manufactures in exchange for corn".

(f) This is teamed, on the only piece on which either of the transfers have so far been seen (a blue and white loving cup, 15.00cm high by 11.25cm diameter), with a print which shows a similar ship, also flying the flag of "Free Trade" lying off shore, while in the foreground Britannia, scroll in hand, discusses a treaty of trade with the 'four continents' expressed in allegoric style. The print is encaptioned "Free trade with all the world".

(g) Last, and perhaps one of the most interesting pieces of the whole Corn Law saga, is a plate commemorating not one of the great heroes but the comparatively minor orator and writer, Colonel Perronet Thompson.

The plate, which is 17.5cm diameter, very poorly printed in black and with a coarse daisy border, shows the Colonel, with his prominent kiss-curl of hair, glowering formidably from a head-and-shoulders portrait. The print is encaptioned simply "Colonel Thompson".

The cause of the Free Trade campaign and/or the celebra-

A matched pair of Scottish soup plates, of George IV and Caroline   Colour Plate 8

tion of its success was further supported by a large number of moulded pieces, usually jugs, carrying on either side portraits of Peel and of Cobden.

There is also, and this is a very rare piece indeed, a very fine rectangular plaque, featuring a black print of Cobden, simply encaptioned "Richard Cobden M.P." and further decorated with sprigs of flowers, the whole plaque being lavishly embellished with pink lustre.

The death of the two heroes, incidentally, was also recorded. There was, however, only one piece known to have been published to mark Cobden's demise. This is a porcelainous mug, of very poor quality, decorated with a black transfer of Cobden and the inscription "Richard Cobden, late M.P. for Rochdale. Born June 29 1804, died April 28 1865." (It is, incidentally, extraordinary that the potter should get both dates wrong. He was born on June the 3rd and died on April the 2nd.)

Peel's sudden death on the other hand was treated as a national catastrophe. The accident happened on Saturday, June the 29th 1850. The *Illustrated London News* of July the 6th reports:

> The scene of the disastrous occurrence was on Constitution Hill, along which the Right Hon. Baronet was riding shortly after five o'clock, at a slow pace, from Buckingham Palace, where he had just made a call. He had arrived nearly opposite the wicket gate leading into the Green Park, when he met Miss Ellis, one of Lady Dover's daughters, on horseback, attended by a groom. Sir Robert had scarcely exchanged salutes when his horse became slightly restive [his favourite bay mare having become too old, Peel had bought this new horse in May]. He was observed for a moment to sit very unsteadily, rolling from side to side, and the next instant the horse turned sharply round and threw Sir Robert over its head upon his face.

A passing doctor, Dr Fourcant, gave immediate assistance. Peel was groaning heavily and said he was 'much hurt'. He was then helped into the carriage of a passer-by, a Mrs Lucas of Bryanston Square, and taken to his house in Whitehall Gardens. He was able to walk from the carriage to the dining-room, but there he collapsed again, and indeed there

227. The least known hero of the Anti-Corn-Law League. Colonel Perronet Thompson was a very minor orator and tract writer. How he came to be featured on this very roughly printed and poorly potted child's plate is a mystery.

228. Although this mug is of very poor quality indeed it is the only piece known to record the death of Cobden, and was, presumably, made as a local rather than a national souvenir.

229. These green dry-ware jugs, appliqué'd with this meticulous white figure of Peel, were made at his death. They come in a range of sizes, and often have metal 'hot-water' lids. On the bottom is printed possibly the worst commemorative poem ever written.

he died at nine minutes past eleven on Tuesday night; apparently from pneumonia caused by a broken fifth rib. He was buried at Drayton Bassett, parish church to Drayton Manor where he had lived.

There was a very considerable number of pieces published to mark the catastrophe. The most often met with, although it is by no means common, is a mug 7.5cm high by 7.5cm diameter, black-rimmed and black-printed with, on the one side a bust portrait of Peel against a vignetted background, the print encaptioned "Sir R. Peel Bart.", and on the other a print of "Drayton Manor", so encaptioned.

Other, and really rather rare, prints are:

(a) A transfer of Sir Robert on horseback, encaptioned "Sir Robert Peel Bart.". This transfer is adapted from a print of Peel which appears in the *Illustrated London News* of July the 6th.

(b) A print of the statesman, looking extraordinarily old and haggard, gazing three-quarters to sinister, in a vignette background; the print encaptioned "Sir Robt Peel".

(c) A print of the statesman in half profile looking to sinister enclosed within an elaborate floral cartouche. This so far has been seen only brown printed on a rococo-handled jug 16.9cm high by 10.6cm diameter the reverse printed with a portrait of Sir Robert on horseback very similar to (a) but with a background clearly indicating this to be a representation of the scene of his accident. On the bottom of the jug, within a wreath cartouche, is printed "Sir R Peel, lamented by an Empire".

(d) A full-face print of the statesman as a young man, set within an elaborately illustrated circular cartouche depicting the achievements of his career, and so encaptioned: "Emancipation", "Corn-Law", "Police"; this above a box cartouche at the base of the portrait in which is inscribed "Sir Robert Peel Born 5th Feb 1788 Died July 2nd 1850".

The inspiration for this transfer comes from the front page of the *Illustrated London News* of July the 12th.

(e) Undoubtedly the most delightful of all Peel memorial pieces: the transfer shows a view of Constitution Hill, complete with pedestrian figures and a figure on horseback and is, almost line for line taken from the issue of the

Illustrated London News that reported Peel's death and achievements on July the 6th. The print is encaptioned "Constitution Hill, the place where Sir Robert Peel met with his fatal accident June 29 1850". The print has so far been seen only on a child's plate, black-printed.

There is also one extremely rare jug, 17.5cm high, of green 'smear' glaze, ornamented with marvellously crisp full-length mouldings of the statesman, on the base of which within an elaborate cartouche of weeping willows is the splendid rhyme "Farewell great statesman!, Long will thy honest worth be missed. In the councils of the Nation. And when the time of England's difficulty comes. Then will the people truly feel The Patriot they have lost in Robert Peel." The jug is marked 'Patent Mosaic', T. & R. Booth.

Very shortly after the passing of the bill the vengeful protectionists had brought Peel down. The actual cause of his downfall was a fairly minor bill, designed to give greater powers in Ireland for the maintenance of law and order. The Whigs joined with the right-wing Tories and voted the

231. The most common of the transfers published to regret the death of Peel. It is more usually found on these rather roughly potted children's plates, often known to exit.

232. This is possibly the rarest of all gin flasks. Not only is it the only form of commemorative for Melbourne recorded, but this particular flask is the only one known to exist.

bill out on its second reading. Three days later Peel resigned.

'If Sir Robert Peel has lost office,' said Cobden at the last meeting of the then defunct Anti-Corn-Law League, on July the 2nd, 'he has gained a country.'

It seems a very apt epitaph on the last great political commemorative splurge of the century.

For, amazingly enough, as far as is known there were no other political upheavals that the potters saw fit to remember. Nothing for the Chartists. Nothing for the Tolpuddle Martyrs. Nothing for the second Great Reform Bill. Nor the various factory acts. Nothing even for the birth of the unions.

But politicians themselves continued to find commemorative favour. Though far fewer of them than one might have thought likely.

There is rumoured to be a salt-glaze gin flask of Palmerston – presumably made, if it does exist, when he was at the height of his popularity as a war-time Premier in the Crimean War.

There is definitely a gin flask of Melbourne. Made, one suspects, at the time of the Ladies of the Bedchamber furore.

And then at 3.25 p.m. on the afternoon of Tuesday, September the 14th 1852 the Duke of Wellington died.

His death was commemorated by a spate of pottery, some of which is of a very high aesthetic standard indeed, in an age when aesthetics were beginning to be sadly lacking in much of the pottery produced. Some of the more remarkable pieces and prints are:

(a) A very finely moulded plaque, sometimes circular in form and sometimes rectangular, decorated in very rich colours and showing the Duke seated on a 'throne' on the base of which is incised "Wellington". This design is taken from a statuette made by 'Alfred Crowquill', showing the Duke in his seat in the House of Lords (hence the 'throne' effect). It was originally produced in pottery as a parian figure by Samuel Alcock and Co. of Burslem, who may, of course, also have made these plaques. These are rare pieces.

(b) A transfer of the Duke in state robes, holding the great sword and posed against a background of St Paul's Cathedral. The print is encaptioned "Wellington as Prime Minister".

(c) A print, encaptioned so, of "Walmer Castle, Kent".

(d) A very 'primitive' transfer (obviously an adaptation

154

233. This transfer has, so far, been recorded only on plates. Note the curious date. On other plates, however, the death date is correctly given.

of an old engraving) of the Duke on horseback, riding through a battle. The print is encaptioned "The Duke at Waterloo".

These last three all appear on one jug and the first two of them appear together on a very finely blue-black-printed mug 7.5cm high by 8.1cm diameter.

(e) A waist-length portrait of Wellington, the old man sitting, full face, his hands clasped together on his knee. The print is encaptioned above the figure, "May I MDCCLXVIIII" and below, "September XIV MDCCCLII". (Note the caption to the plate above. The transfer may have been torn while being applied.)

(f) A full-length portrait, showing the old man seated in a 'dining' chair, in profile looking to sinister, with, behind him on an ornamental ledge, a statuette of Napoleon. The print is simply encaptioned "Wellington". This print has so far been found only on a saucer, black printed, and with a widespread rim decoration in blue and on a jug from the

234. Another transfer that owes its inspiration to the *Illustrated London News*. There are three popular transfers featuring Wellington at Waterloo. Far too often these are offered as souvenirs of Waterloo, whereas, of course, all were published at the time of Wellington's death.

235. The death of the Iron Duke produced a spate of different transfers. This, and the other very similar ones featuring the Duke and his achievements, are usually found on jugs of this shape printed in either black or red or purple, and in at least one instance marked for R. Cochran & Co. of Verreville Pottery, Glasgow.

same tea service. There must, of course, be a cup. What it has on it is still unknown.

(g) A representation of the Duke on the field of Waterloo, riding his famous charger Copenhagen and waving his troops forward with a gesture of his cocked hat in his right hand, the scene encaptioned "Up guards and at them!" This is set within a circular cartouche in which is written "Duke of Wellington. Born 30 April 1769. Assaye. Waterloo. Died 14 Sep 1852". The print has so far been seen only on daisy plates, of various sizes, printed in blue.

(h) A transfer of the Duke in very similar stance to (g), but in this transfer flanked by field officers and with a wave of cheering troops behind him: the print is encaptioned, above, "Waterloo" and below, "Up guards and at them".

(i) An elaborate design showing the head of the young Wellington in a circular cartouche, topped by the British lion and flanked either side by an arrangement of flags and banners emblazoned with the names of his victories, the print further adorned by the weapons of war.

156

(j) An elaborate design showing the head of the old Duke in an oval cartouche, topped by a ducal coronet and, within a ribbon cartouche, at the bottom the word "Wellington". This flanked on either side by an arrangement of standards emblazoned with his victories. The whole design further embellished with martial symbols.

And, once the Duke was dead, that was that. As has been said, the potters, curiously enough, did not revive any interest in any particular happening political for the rest of the century.

There were, however, a number of pieces made to commemorate certain individual statesmen, and some of the more important of these are now listed:

John Bright – of Corn Law fame. Of him there is only one known transfer. This shows an almost full-face of the statesman, bearded and in late Victorian dress. The print fades out to vignette background. The print is sometimes seen teamed with a print of Gladstone, or with a print, so encaptioned, of "One Ash Mr · John Bright's House at Rochdale".

Joseph Chamberlain – the Republican turned Tory. He was commemorated on one of the series of 23.75cm octagonal plates which are very freely available and which were produced to honour quite a number of late Victorian public figures.

Benjamin Disraeli – Prime Minister in 1867 and 1874. Dizzy is widely commemorated on a number of pieces. The most easily found are octagonal plates, either black-transferred or black-printed and further embellished with green and yellow, the latter often used to stress the primroses which adorn the print.

William Ewart Gladstone – Disraeli's main Parliamentary opponent. Both Gladstone and Mrs Gladstone are freely commemorated. Both appear on a whole series of matched plates, rather charmingly decorated, often in a brown transfer. (A Doulton jug commemorating the Leeds election and Gladstone does not, of course, refer to William Ewart, but to his son.)

Stafford Henry Northcote, 1st Earl of Iddesleigh – a notable Conservative politician who died, suddenly, at 10 Downing Street on January the 11th 1887.

236. Transfers of Bright, another Corn Law notable, are rare. They occur on both mugs and loving-cups, usually black-printed, but sometimes printed in a rather reddish brown.

237. Benjamin Disraeli appears on a very wide range of ware indeed: this is, comparatively, an unusual octagonal plate; the more common ones are far more lavishly decorated, often having the primroses clobbered in yellow.

157

238. A very handsome cup regretting the death of Gladstone.

239. Lord Iddesleigh was a notable Conservative politician. He died, very suddenly, actually at 10 Downing Street, in 1887.

240. Lord Salisbury in the full flush of Victorian splendour.

241. Most of these octagonal plates are definitely 'in memoriam'. This one, however, records the short-lived appointment of Randolph Churchill as Chancellor of the Exchequer in 1886.

The Earl is commemorated on yet another of these 23.75cm diameter plates. His portrait shows him with a huge and marvellously Victorian beard, and is encaptioned "In Memoriam", "The Rt Hon the Earl of Iddesleigh".

Charles Stewart Parnell – the great Irish reformer. He is yet another subject to be found on the octagonal 23.75cm diameter series of plates. And this is far and away the most common piece commemorating him. There are, however, also some quite rare Parnell 'gin' flasks. These can be found either in imitation salt-glaze, or as overglaze-decorated, rather rough pot. They mirror, in form, the much earlier flasks of the 1830s.

Lord Randolph Churchill – Third son of the 7th Duke of Marlborough and a Conservative politician. He was Chancellor of the Exchequer and Leader of the House from July to December 1886, an achievement commemorated by yet another octagonal plate, carrying his portrait and the inscription "Lord Randolph Churchill, Chancellor of the Exchequer 1886".

158

5
A Note on Railways

Of all the great engineering events of the nineteenth century the coming of the railways certainly created both the most change and the most excitement. Consequently, from 1830 on, a huge quantity of railway ware was produced.

Little of this, however, is genuinely commemorative. Most of it is brown-printed, most commonly on mugs, usually overglaze-clobbered, and features a surprisingly limited range of four- and six-wheeled engines variously named, without any apparent rhyme or reason, *Deakin*, *Jaco* (presumably, in fact, the *Iago*) *Express*, *Mail*, *Nero* (or *Hero*), *Fury*, *Wooda*. Some, at least, of these mugs are marked "Railway J & R" for J. & R. Godwin of Cobridge, Staffordshire.

There is little doubt that this ware was produced right up to the end of the nineteenth century; although it is reasonable to assume that most of it would have been made in the two great periods of railway boom.

Certain specific events were, however, commemorated.

The first, and far and away the most celebrated of these, was the opening in 1830 of Britain's first genuine 'railway', running from Liverpool to Manchester. (The Stockton/ Darlington was opened in 1825. It was not, however, in the modern sense, truly a 'railway', as in certain places it still relied on the pull of static engines.)

But on September the 15th 1830 the Prime Minister, his Grace the Duke of Wellington, opened the Liverpool/ Manchester Line.

The idea of linking the great manufacturing centre of Manchester with the great port of Liverpool had been thought of as early as 1822. There was, however, considerable opposition to the scheme and it was not until four years later that George Stephenson started work on the project.

There were, in the construction of this railway, two engineering miracles. The first was the 'floating' of the permanent way across the four-mile waste of Chat Moss, a

242. One of the most comprehensive railway souvenirs ever transferred. This shaving set carries prints of both the *Rocket* and the *Northumbrian* – Stephenson won the Rainhill trials with the former, and himself drove the latter at the opening ceremony of the Liverpool/Manchester railway on September the 15th 1830. By courtesy of the City of Liverpool Museums.

barren bog near the Manchester end. The other was the Edge Hill Tunnel, which took the line actually under the town of Liverpool, to debouch at the Liverpool docks. This had, at one end of it, the famous and much-illustrated Moorish Arch.

But before the railroad opened there was all the excitement of the celebrated Rainhill locomotive trials. These took place on October the 6th 1829. There were, originally, five engines entered; the *Rocket*, built by George Stephenson; the *Novelty*, built by Braithwaite and Ericson; the *Sans Pareil*, built by Hackworth; the *Perseverance* and the *Cyclopeda*. The last two could reach only 6 m.p.h. and were withdrawn. The *Sans Pareil* was found to be $5\frac{1}{2}$ cwt overweight and was disqualified.

Judging by the amount of *Novelty* engines that are shown on transfers and the total rarity of *Rockets*, there is no doubt which engine the potters confidently expected to win.

They were wrong.

243. The 'classic' transfer produced for the opening of the Liverpool/Manchester line: this print appears on both mug and jugs. It is interesting to see that the potters thought the Braithwaite-Ericson engine had far greater possibilities than Stephenson's Rainhill entry.

The *Novelty* was certainly the faster of the two engines. But she was so beset with mechanical mishaps that eventually she too was withdrawn. And the prize went to the *Rocket*. (If you want to see her, she stands today in the Science Museum, South Kensington.)

And so, on that celebrated day in 1830, the railway was finally opened. The ducal party duly embarked on a three-carriage train drawn by the *Northumbrian* and driven by George Stephenson himself, and set out for Manchester, complete with all the dignitaries of the city and the railway and a hugely clamorous brass band.

The occasion however, was sadly marred by the death of Mr Huskisson, President of the Board of Trade, who was run down at the Parkfield halt and who died the same day. Indeed, it was only after great persuasion that the Duke agreed to proceed and the railway was opened at all.

161

Not only do nearly all the pieces published show the wrong engine, they also without exception fail to mention poor Mr Huskisson at all.

So, while there is absolutely no doubt that all of them were genuinely made for the opening, there is equally no doubt that the majority of the plates must have been engraved before the Rainhill trials.

Indeed, there were only two transfers used. The one is really very rare, and even the other is by no means a thing one comes across every day.

The transfers are, in inverse order of rarity:

A view of the Moorish Arch, with two engines in the foreground and a considerable number of spectators standing round. The print is encaptioned "Entrance to the Liverpool Manchester Railway". This is always coupled with a print showing the *Novelty* pulling an open coach and a wagon loaded with barrels. This pair of prints can be found on both mugs and jugs, printed in blue, black or purple.

A close-up of the *Northumbrian* pulling a tender and two carriages. In the first carriage is a band and in the second the various dignitaries attendant on the opening ceremony. The print has, so far, been seen only on jugs and always printed in black. The jugs are marked, on the base, "Liverpool & Manchester Railway".

Surprisingly enough, when one considers the fantastic railway boom of the mid-'30s and mid-'40s and the great quantity of general railway ware produced, only one other railway opening seems to have been commemorated on pottery. This was the Sheffield and Rotherham Railway which was opened by Earl Fitzwilliam on October the 31st 1838.

For this opening there are only two pieces known to have been published; a simply splendid mug and jug, now in the Rotherham Museum. Both are blue-printed, with a very fine view of an engine and train crossing a river bridge. The print is encaptioned above the picture, "Sheffield Rotherham Railway opened October 31 1838".

However, two other railway events caught the interest of certain potters. The first was the introduction of United States engines. This took place on the Birmingham/Gloucester

railway, when it was opened in September 1840. Believing that no British engine could surmount the notorious Lickey Incline, a two-mile climb of 1 in $37\frac{1}{2}$ from Bromsgrove to Blackwell, Captain Moorson, the railway's engineer, ordered seventeen special locomotives from Norris & Co of Philadelphia. There is a rare plate, 26.25cm diameter, commemorating this event, showing one of the Norris engines, patriotically flying a Union Jack, crossing a very impressive viaduct. The plate is uncaptioned.

The second was the start of 'official' mail-runs by the railways, in 1838. Mail had been carried by the railways since they began. But not altogether harmoniously. So, in August 1838, the Government passed an act to make this traffic official; actually 'requiring' the companies, and any new companies to come, to carry the mails. The terms laid down were strict.

Separate mail vans were to be used. Mobile sorting offices could be required. Staff were enumerated. Terms were set. Regularity of services was insisted on. From this day on the Royal Mail and the railways were indivisibly set together.

Whether one can claim that this event was specifically 'commemorated' or not is open to question; but there certainly were a number of pieces published showing the London to Liverpool mail coach in a train containing the two other coaches 'Victoria' and 'Coronation', which clearly dates it at 1838.

The transfer has, so far, been seen printed only in blue and usually very well defined. The engine name varies – the two versions known are *London* and *Liverpool*, and the engine is of the four-wheel class, very similar to the one now on show in the Liverpool Museum, and quite clearly intended to be a representation of that. The elaborate, first-class, coaches are marked in order, 'Victoria', 'Coronation', then 'London Royal Mail Liverpool', without the coat of arms which the act permitted to be used, but with an outside guard perched up behind. The train ends with a flat truck carrying a private carriage. It is travelling through the typical, mythical, rather mountainous rural scenery often seen on general railway ware.

There are two other railway transfers which, just, scrape into the commemorative class. Both are connected with the opening of the Liverpool/Manchester railway, and both show engines which arrived too late to take part in the opening celebrations. These engines were the *William the Fourth* and *Queen Adelaide*, built in 1830 by Braithwaite and Ericson.

The transfer of the *William the Fourth* shows the engine in great detail, pulling three third-class carriages. It has, so far, been found only on a mug 10.00cm high by 10.00cm diameter, printed in pink.

The transfer of the *Adelaide* is less satisfactory. This has been seen only on a very poorly printed Leeds mug, 8.25cm high, transferred in reddish-brown and overglaze-enamelled, with a print that though marked "Adelaide" looks suspiciously like the *Novelty*. The print is encaptioned "Liverpool & Manchester Railway".

Considerably later in time, but still within the limits of

this book, is a transfer commemorating the centenary of George Stephenson's birth. The commemorative pieces which are, as far as the authors know, all mugs, are either waisted or straight-sided, printed in black with, on the one side, a rather coarse head-and-shoulders portrait of the engineer, encaptioned "George Stephenson", and on the other "N.E.R. locomotive No 925" (an E. Fletcher Express Goods engine) which took first prize for the best-decorated engine at the grand celebrations in Newcastle.

Lastly, there are four specific transfers which are sufficiently individual to justify inclusion. These show:

(a) An unidentified engine crossing a bridge over a river. Amongst the coaches is one with the royal crown on its roof. There is no clue as to where the scene is set, or, indeed, which line is shown. However, the carriage is from its shape certainly not Queen Adelaide's, and therefore by process of elimination

246. The *London* engine pulling a mail train. This transfer was made in Coronation year, 1838, and commemorates the start of 'official' mail-runs. An alternative but exactly similar print has the engine named *Liverpool*.

must be one of the carriages made for Victoria. So the only certain thing is that the print must have been published after June the 18th 1842 – the day on which the first royal trip was made, from Slough to Paddington.

(b) A fine view of the *Rocket* pulling a simple tender. The print is encaptioned "The Rocket of Messrs R Stephenson". Perhaps the finest example can be seen, brown printed, on a shaving set now housed in the Liverpool Museum.

(c) Included because it is the only Scottish railway piece the authors have ever seen: on a mug 12.75cm diameter by 9.50cm high, blue-printed, the engine *Caledonian* pulling three carriages across a bridge. Also included in the transfer are a harbour with a sailing ship and a steam packet and a number of men harvesting. The print is encaptioned "Success to the Rail, the Shuttle & Flail" and the mug is marked "Albion".

(d) A very early engine passing a rather splendid country house. This is, almost certainly, Blenkinsop's train on the Brandling Junction railway, passing the house of Mr Arthing-

247. A very rare print of the Braithwaite and Ericson engine *William the Fourth*: this engine was ordered for the Manchester/Liverpool line, but was delivered too late to take part in the opening ceremony. It was not a success and was later sold and used on the construction of the North Union railway.

ton, the brewer. This has been seen only on a blue-and-white printed jug, 22.86cm by 13.97cm diameter, presumably published in 1812 which would, on current knowledge, make this the earliest railway transfer published. (This coal-carrying railway was built in 1812, for Charles Brandling, M.P., on the instructions of John Blenkinsop of the colliery, who also designed the engine. There were two rack engines employed, the *Prince Regent* and the *Salamanca*.)

6

What to See and Where to See it

However well pieces are described, or however good the photographs, nothing can compare with actually seeing them and preferably, handling them.

To see much commemorative ware is, unfortunately, not all that easy. Few museums have extensive collections and all too often the commemoratives they do have are in what is euphemistically called their 'reserve collections'; which means they are in a store cupboard and can only be seen if advance notice is given.

There is really only one museum which is worth a special visit. This is the Brighton Museum. For in it is housed the quite fabulous Willett Collection.

The late Mr Willett spent much of a long life building up this astounding collection of documentary pottery. Regrettably much of it is not on permanent show. But there are two rooms full of exhibits, many of them pertinent to this period, which are always open. And the curator and his staff are most helpful to any serious collector who wants to go behind the scenes.

You will find the Museum by the side of the Pavilion. When you have seen it, visit the Pavilion itself. In it and always on show there is a small but excellent collection of pieces appertaining to George IV, Caroline and Charlotte.

Apart from the Willett there is also quite a number of museums which will certainly repay a visit if you are in their area.

In **London,** go to the London Museum in Kensington Palace. Apart from having the earliest commemorative pot recorded, it has some excellent Victoriana. Go also to the Victoria and Albert, which has a small number of very interesting pieces in the main English pottery room and a

further selection in the Schreiber Collection immediately opposite. The National Maritime Museum at **Greenwich** is also worth a visit for Nelsonia: but the amount of pottery is disappointingly small.

Out of London, and working down from the North, both **Glasgow** and **Edinburgh** are worth seeing. **Sunderland** has a very good museum of lustre; there are not many commemorative pieces in it but it is definitely worth a visit if you're passing. **Preston** has the Harris Museum; this is worth a visit if only to see its George IV Coronation mug. You will however have to give advance notice to the curator. The **Liverpool** Museum has surprisingly little on show, but an excellent collection in store. **Warrington** is a small museum, but it does have its pieces beautifully displayed and in its reserve collection has at least two very rare things. **Manchester,** second to the Willett, probably has the biggest commemorative collection of all. But little is on show – a prior arrangement is most necessary. **Sheffield** has some very interesting local pieces; and a worthwhile amount is almost always on display. For railways enthusiasts, **Rotherham**'s

249. A marvellous blue and white printed jug showing the earliest railway yet recorded, the Brandling Junction colliery line. This particular jug, which is in the famous Elton Collection, carries the only recorded example of the transfer.

tiny museum houses one of the rarest pieces the authors know of; there is nothing else there but this mug alone makes a trip worthwhile. **Epworth** has an excellent Wesley Museum. The Fitzwilliam in **Cambridge** is certainly worth seeing. **Cheltenham** has a small number of pieces, also the **Bristol** Art Gallery is worth a visit, and the near-by Holburne Museum in **Bath** houses the Sir Sydney Barratt Collection; this is a small collection but an extremely interesting one. The National Museum of Wales in **Cardiff** has a mass of Swansea and Glamorgan pottery, amongst which is a small amount of very interesting commemorative ware. **Monmouth** has the Nelson Museum; little pottery but worth seeing for its splendid documentation.

Obviously any local museum can prove unexpectedly worthwhile. The authors have not, they are sure, visited every one in the United Kingdom and there may certainly be some totally unrecorded commemorative pieces tucked away in small museums. But the listed ones certainly do contain most, if not all, the major known pieces.

7

The Commemorative Calendar

A handy date reference to the main events ceramically commemorated.

1780	Rodney's victory at Cape St Vincent
1781	Cornwallis surrenders at Yorktown
1782	Rodney and Hood win the Battle of the Saintes
1782	Elliot defends Gibraltar
1788	King George III goes mad
1793	War declared by France; Duke of York takes Valenciennes
1794	The Glorious First of June
1797	Battles of St Vincent and of Camperdown
1798	Nelson and the Nile
1800	Pitt's Act of Union
1801	Nelson and Copenhagen
1801–2	Peace of Amiens
1803	War breaks out again
1805	Trafalgar
1809	The Grand National Jubilee and the death of Moore at Corunna
1809–14	The Campaigns of Wellington
1810	Sir Francis Burdett is arrested
1815	Waterloo
1816	Princess Charlotte marries
1817	Princess Charlotte dies
1819	Peterloo
1820	The Duke of Kent dies, as does George III. The Prince Regent becomes George IV and Caroline is 'tried' under the Bill of Pains and Penalties
1821	The Coronation of George IV; the death of Queen Caroline
1822	George IV visits Scotland
1827	The Duke of York dies

1828	O'Connell elected M.P. for the County of Clare
1830	George IV dies. William IV accedes
1831	William IV and Queen Adelaide crowned
1832	The Reform Bill is passed
1833	The Anti-Slavery Bill is passed
1837	William IV dies. Victoria succeeds to the Throne
1838	Victoria is crowned
1840	Victoria and Albert are married and later that year the Princess Royal is born
1841	The Prince of Wales is born
1846	The Corn Laws are repealed
1850	Sir Robert Peel dies
1851	The Great Exhibition
1852	The Duke of Wellington dies
1854	The Crimean War begins; the battles of Alma, Balaklava and Inkerman take place
1855	Sebastopol is taken
1856	Peace is signed
1857	General Havelock dies in the Indian Mutiny
1858	The Princess Royal marries
1860	The Prince of Wales visits Canada, the Queen reviews the Volunteers
1861	Albert dies
1863	The Prince of Wales marries
1885	Gordon is killed in Khartoum
1887	The Golden Jubilee
1897	The Diamond Jubilee

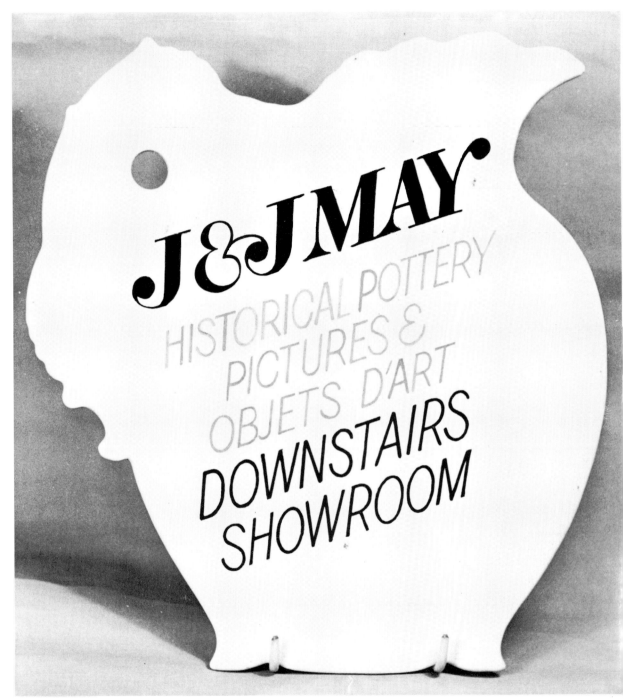

250. A personal commemorative: this has been the shop sign of J. & J. May ever since they started business and is now in the window of the shop at 40 Kensington Church Street, London.

Index

Index

(Numbers in brackets refer to pictures or picture captions)